"The late Dr. Ferrol Sams said the secret to solid writing is simple: Find a good story, then tell it well. With *Helen's Untold Story*, Hue Rainey has found a *great* one that he shares beautifully. As the sole survivor of the tragic balloon crash that altered Helen's history forever, he can tell the story of Alpine Helen because he lived it. With words straight from the heart, Rainey gives us a firsthand—even intimate—look at this significant slice of North Georgia's history. Well done!"

—*Emory Jones*
Author, The Valley Where They Danced

"Hue Rainey has given us the real 'inside look' at the founding of Alpine Helen. It truly is an untold story, and only Hue could have told it. Thankfully, his memories are vivid. I love this book."

—*Billy Chism*
Former Editor and Publisher, White County News

3-7-24

Enjoy!

Thanks,

Helen's Untold Story

HOW ONE MAN'S DREAMS AND GAMES BECAME HELEN'S REALITY

HUE RAINEY

MOUNTAIN ARBOR
PRESS
Alpharetta, GA

The author has tried to recreate events, locations, and conversations from his memories of them. The author has made every effort to give credit to the source of any images, quotes, or other material contained within and obtain permissions when feasible.

Copyright © 2019 by Hue Rainey

All rights reserved. No part of this book may be reproduced or transmitted in any form or by any means, electronic or mechanical, including photocopying, recording, or any information storage and retrieval system, without permission in writing from the author.

ISBN: 978-1-63183-516-2 - Paperback
eISBN: 978-1-63183-517-9 - ePub
eISBN: 978-1-63183-518-6 - mobi

Library of Congress Control Number: 2019939286

Printed in the United States of America   0 4 1 7 1 9

∞This paper meets the requirements of ANSI/NISO Z39.48-1992 (Permanence of Paper)

This book is dedicated to all the wonderful folks that came to Alpine Helen and became part of Pete's puzzle with their dreams and excitement. Their involvement in Helen enriched their lives and led Helen to be what it is today: a Bavarian dreamworld in the Northeast Georgia mountains. They are the reason others have come to push Helen forward as a leader in Georgia and national tourism.

If they are still alive, they should be proud; and if not, may their survivors be proud of them. They made a difference.

Pete—a free spirit who frequently soared above the rest of us, both in imagination and courage. He delighted in repeating the observation that mountain ballooning, with its hazardous terrain and air currents, was a perfect analogy for the adventurous spirit that could prod a small town like Helen to pull itself up by its own bootstraps. We do not have to erect a statue to Pete. The City of Helen is his monument.

—Phil Garner (as reported in the *Mountain Eagle*, May 1976)

Contents

Foreword	xi
Preface	xiii
Acknowledgments	xix
Introduction	xxi
SUMMER 1975	1
In the Beginning	3
He's Not Butch, He's My Brother	17
Bavarian Brook Golf Course and Racquet Club	23
NOTABLES	29
The Good Old Boys	31
The Eagle Did Fly	37
FALL 1975	39
Pete's Nowhere? It's Nowhere to Be Found	41
Chamber of Commerce	45
The Secrets of Hilltop House	49
Dreams and Corporations	53
Early-Morning Return	57
Where Did You Say the Chattahoochee Started?	61
NOTABLES	67
Chief	69
Sharing His Candy	77
WINTER 1975–1976	83
The Story of the Village Inn	85

The Devil Made Us Do It	91
Crazy!	93
Gold Spikes Impress German Metal Working Horn Tooter	95
Spare Tire and All, Including the Jackass	99
Helen's Atlantic	101
NOTABLES	105
Doctor Tom	107
SPRING 1976	111
We Believe in Our Carousel	113
The Great Easter-Olive Hunt	115
Developers, Not Promoters!	117
The Great Bike Race	125
Helen to Atlanta, the Old-Fashioned Way	131
A YEAR END	137
Our Balloon Burst	139
What If?	151
The End or Beginning	153

Foreword

Herzlich willkommen!

A hearty welcome to you from Georgia's Alpine village, Helen. The first impression people get when they enter Helen is that they have somehow stepped in a Bavarian village right in the middle of the Georgia mountains. And that's exactly the feeling we want to perpetuate. Helen is an impression of a Bavarian village. We do not pretend to be an authentic German town. However, if losing yourself for a few hours or days in a town that imparts a feeling of being in Europe is appealing; if you like seeing glassware, candles, candy, and woodcrafts produced before your eyes; if you enjoy balloon rides, clogging, live theater, and authentic German festivals; then, you're going to love Helen. We offer all this and more.

One of the most frequently asked questions is, "How did this town get started?" Elsewhere in other publications, you will find what is pretty much the accepted version of the "Helen story." But there is so much more to the story. If getting Helen started was difficult, keeping it going with so many people continuing in the same direction might have been impossible without a strong-willed dreamer: Peter Hodkinson III. When things went wrong, Pete had an answer. When Helen needed something to attract tourists, Pete had an idea. When the press needed a story, Pete had one or created one; and all the time he would tell you (with his tongue deep in his cheek), this was all impossible. "There can't be a town like this in Georgia."

Pete was instrumental in starting the first theater in Helen featuring *The Sound of Music*, the Helen to the Atlantic Balloon Race, a golf course (now gone, but plans are in the wings for another course), and a thousand other projects that helped make Helen what it is today. He operated the International House as a showcase of what he thought a gift shop should be, and the Wurst Haus, a restaurant he then owned, was the center of activities in town. He hosted several Oktoberfests there until that event became tent-sized and now is housed in our pavilion.

Pete taught us how to be a tourist town, and then he died tragically in a balloon accident in 1976 while promoting an event and a town that were both so important to him. When he died, people thought Helen might fade, but he taught us too well. The spirit of Pete lives today in so many whose lives he touched and some he never knew. It's embodied in Winston Lusk, balloon pilot; Mervin Fried of the Old Norway shop; Lanier Chambers, realtor; Roy Sims, former mayor and a builder; Hue Rainey, motel operator; Jim Wilkins, land owner and developer; Dave Jones, candymaker; and so many more. That's the "real" story of Helen. It's what we are and why we are. Tourist trap? Hardly. Overcommercialized? I think not.

We are here for you to have a good time. We are affordable, ever-changing, and unique. Enjoy us.

—Written in 1982 by then Helen Chamber of Commerce President David Jones, owner and operator of Hansel & Gretel Candy Kitchen with wife Janet since 1973

Preface

For nearly forty-three years, I have lived with a haunting truth and realization about a simple faith born in Helen, Georgia. As a major tourist area, the Alpine village's beginning is as unusual as it is quaint. The haunting truth I refer to is totally from my personal experiences, and therefore is my personal opinion. I have heard it said there is one thing about opinions: everybody seems to have one. And that's about what they are worth: plentiful, common, and as varied as the people who have them. In the case of my opinion, I have a burning desire to document it, which is something that is out of the ordinary for me. In deciding whether to write for my own personal archives or for public documentation, I prefer to share with others for several reasons, some more important than others. The haunting truth? It is that dreams must sometimes be pulled out of you before you even know they are in there.

Over the years, many have enjoyed and bragged on our little Alpine village, but as you might expect, there have also been some negative comments. It is my nature to let negativism slide, but sometimes it's more than I can handle. On those occasions, I find myself getting defensive, which goes against my grain. In defense of the existence of Helen, I feel that the undesirable comments are of no consequence, because the people offering them haven't a clue. It is my belief that negativism is just like an opinion—not worth much. Sharing a short period of my personal life that gives a totally different view of the making and success of Helen seemed like a good way to refute the naysayers, to me. And so, you hold in your hand my first attempt to preserve history for future posterity.

When reaching for a previously unheard-of dream, there are usually core beliefs and backgrounds that push to the surface to obtain a direction that will produce success. In most unlikely success stories, there is a special person who leads the way. These kinds of remarkable leaders are all different; they are made from a different mold, made of different stuff, and cut from a different kind of cloth. They guide a project in their own unique way. Many will lead by committee and seek the support of large corporations, governmental support, and money from large investors. A few lead by dreams, some by games and manipulation. There are very few who have the ability to pull what they need from little everyday people, who, somewhere in their subconscious, have their own dreams. It is a rare leader who can overlook folks' shortcomings while, at the same time, pulling their giving qualities to surface. This trait works beautifully with salt-of-the-earth folks so as to fit them into a plan of development that produces both success and completion.

I knew such a leader once! Only once, in my lifetime to date, have I ever known a person with such dynamic leadership qualities. You may or may not have known him or ever even heard of him; however, when you round the curve heading into the city limits of Helen, you come face to face with his creation. Once you are within the city limits, you are caught in the dreamworld of a visionary, one who pulled personal dreams out of normal people from all walks of life in order to plug them into his master developmental puzzle. The results were, numerous dreams came true, and the completed puzzle, Helen, Georgia, was recreated into an Alpine village.

Helen's Untold Story

Pete Hodkinson was my friend from the first time I met him in June of 1975 until his last living breath in May 1976. His last words to me came as we stared eye to eye less than fifty feet from the electrical trunk line that fed power to all of Toccoa, Georgia. It all started when Pete simply asked me, "Hue, you ready for your first balloon flight?"

Having no idea that it would be his last, my reply was, "Sure, let's go."

He spoke his last words to me some hour and a half later as we were trying to land on the other side of Toccoa. For some unknown reason, the hot-air balloon wouldn't lift and gain enough altitude to clear the power lines. Pete was doing all he could to clear the lines, but when he saw it was fruitless, he said to me, "Get down the rope." Those words would be his last, as without question I turned, putting my hand on the side of the basket, and jumped over the side.

The result for me, at age thirty-two, was another chance at life. My friend Pete, who was a true free spirit and lived his life on the edge, didn't survive this time. His death that May was of shocking proportion. I had lost a friend and mentor. Yet, as the years passed, it strengthened my respect for the dream and my desire to always remember how and why we would succeed in Helen.

Pete created the puzzle. He led the way. He awakened our early desires and abilities to do our little parts to create one of the most unlikely and unusual tourist areas in all of America, and maybe the world. I'll not go deep into the background of my friend. I have decided that his life growing up was quite complex, and deserves documentation of its own to give a complete accounting of his interesting early years. I will say he came from a remarkable background from the Far East to Scotland, stretching from the North all the way to South Georgia. He lost his parents in as tragic a way as he himself died. Of course, his death would have been as he might have wanted it: pushing the envelope and doing what he enjoyed. He challenged life and lived it as a game.

For Pete, dreams and fantasies were only something to accomplish. I never heard him say the words, "I wish we could." If he wished it, he would find a way to accomplish it. As for me, I was a player with a dream that he awakened. Joining my grandfather and father, Pete became one of three mentors that were significant in my life. My grandfather gave me my basics in faith and relationship with God. Dad, whom I loved dearly, was also my best friend. He raised me, giving me the everyday values that molded my life. Then came Pete. Pete taught me that dreams are something to challenge, not to let lie in wait for "someday." He taught me there's always a way to obtain a goal. This is my attempt to pay tribute to him, his larger-than-life personality, and his vision.

It is my hope that this little book will open your eyes to the real Helen, as Pete meant it to be. Sure, over the years it's gotten sidetracked a little, and it's not quite the way it started, but progress brings change every place it goes. It happens to the best of them. Maybe you will see the real Helen as it was meant to be (and still is in some places). Much heart and heartbreak went into the recreation of the town. Our hearts were in it all the way, and I think that will show among the stories in the following pages. This written record is important to the ones of us that still remain, as well as a remembrance of the many who have gone.

I want you to enjoy a one-year journey through my life and the life of some of my friends—how we came to Helen, how we played the game, and how we followed the man that led us. It was fun like none of us had ever had, before or since. And maybe, just maybe, the stories will inspire a dream inside of you. Maybe you will ask yourself, "Am I doing what I want? Is there something more to my life?" Maybe a spark will be lit and a dream will become more than a dream by transforming into reality. My grandmamma had a simple saying she used to tell us kids: "Can't can't do nothing!" She was a woman of wisdom who knew the truth and wasn't afraid to speak it.

I ask you to get something personal out of this book. Take that something with you through your later life. I sure have taken a lot from living it. My wife and friends who read this manuscript asked me, "How do you remember all these stories after forty-three years?"

I say, "When you accomplish and live a dream, it's not hard. It's never forgotten."

Acknowledgments

Many thanks to those that have waited so long for me to finally have this book published. All of you know who you are, and I'm so sorry it dragged on for over sixteen years. The time had to be right, and the fiftieth anniversary of Alpine Helen is that time.

Thank you to Michelle Gunnin for your support and guidance with the book format and assistance with editing. To Billy Chism for encouraging me to get on with it and get this book published. To Emory Jones for kind words of encouragement, helpful hints, and introducing me to the publisher. Without these three individuals, this book would still be in the file cabinet.

And, to my readers. Thank you in advance for reading my book about this year in Helen. I hope you gain understanding of what can be done by dreams and games resulting in reality. I hope it will show you a positive future direction in life to come.

And, a special thank-you to my wife, Jane, who has supported me in this unlikely adventure and challenge. Although she didn't live this era with me, she is a local girl whose dad, Wicky, and mother, Cissy, were early supporters of me. Jane, her brother, Bill, and sister, Susan, all worked in Helen in those early days. I love you all, but Jane is so special to me.

Introduction

Ever since my battle with cancer, I've tried to visit Colorado in the winter for a ski holiday every year. This tradition began in April of 1979, when I decided that I was really going to live. After a year consisting of two operations and three months of killer chemo, which had dropped my weight from 215 lbs. to 143 lbs. in three months' time, my goal was to regain my quality of life. I was left with no hair, no appetite, a damaged kidney, very little use of my left hand, and many more unpleasant side effects. More importantly, despite all the terrible parts of treatment, I was blessed to have been left with my life. The doctors at Emory, my family, and my friends had literally saved my life. Of course, I didn't quit fighting either. It was a team effort. I was only thirty-three years old and had two young daughters that I wanted to see into adulthood. Now, many years later, it's grandkid time, and I've got a whole new set of goals.

Once I was better, I felt I needed a reward for surviving. The late winter and early spring of '79 found me with very little money and a burning desire to go west. It just so happened that during that period in history, gold and silver went crazy, reaching new heights in value. I found a cheap package to Copper Mountain, Colorado, for five days and nights of spring skiing. That's not all I found. I also came across my old gold wedding band, gold high-school ring, gold charms, gold coins, silver flatware, and collector money. All this stuff wasn't doing a damn thing for me, so I stuffed it all in a bag and headed to Northlake Mall to a gold-and-silver collector's shop to see what my junk was worth in real dollars. Turns out, it converted into plenty of funds to reward myself at Copper Mountain.

It was a fabulous trip. I have memories of getting into the heated outside pool at night while the snow floated down on to my quarter inch of new hair. It was wonderful, as was the whole vacation. It was not only my first visit to Colorado, but also my first visit to Vail. Later, both would become important parts of my life. I treated myself to that vacation in Colorado to celebrate being alive by enjoying the Rocky Mountains. While there, I took a drive over Vail Pass to see the up-and-coming ski village, which was the premiere ski spot in America. Unknown to me at the time, this visit would mark a long and important connection to Vail which continues to impact me even now.

In 1983, I bought a resale timeshare penthouse in the Lionshead area of Vail and became a resident (three weeks per year). Every year at Thanksgiving, I've spent all—or at least most—of my three weeks enjoying the area and skiing the one-of-a-kind mountain. It wasn't long before I found I was getting much more than just a fun visit out of my holiday. I began meeting folks who were very successful in life or even famous, some at Rotary make-up meetings. I also found myself observing how an idea thought up by Pete Siebert and Earl Eadten back in the fifties worked and grew. What was once a backcountry sheep ranch and a wilderness mountain area had been visualized, promoted, and developed by these two into a ski area that was brought forward by so many who came later.

In looking around Vail, I found books, videos, memorials, and monuments that kept both the oldest and newest visitors aware of how Vail was created. They recognized who had played the large and small roles in its growth. It was the history of how this jewel in the Rockies came to be and all the materials gave credit where credit was due for its development.

I asked myself why we hadn't done this type of thing in Helen. Nobody really knew how Helen came to be, and more importantly, who led the way. There was no clue why folks had the opportunity to fail or succeed in business in this remote mountain town. Something so simple could make such a difference in how a person might look at their opportunity to be a part of such a unique little place in North Georgia. Maybe knowing why they were able to be here by knowing the history would give them a different approach and make a difference in their happiness in Helen.

Helen didn't just happen randomly. Like Vail, many folks chased a dream and gave of themselves. Vail and Helen are alike in so many ways, not the least of which is that both of their original promoters and developers were free spirits and shared the name Pete. Both were also lucky to be alive, and therefore lived life to the fullest.

I've known for years that the real story of Helen should be told, but no one has taken on the project. Several folks have written about the area and its history, and touched on Helen as you see it today, but they've only touched lightly. The story you are reading covers a one-year period of my personal observation as a part of Helen's beginning. It's so simple, but also so unbelievable that something so far-fetched was real.

I once heard it said by the one who knew best, "Helen isn't typical, and if a person isn't mature and ready for it, keeping everything in perspective, it could be dangerous for them to be involved."

It truly was a pretend world that became reality. It was

a major leader in Georgia's tourist industry by 1975. Only six years after its conception, it became one of the top-five tourist areas in Georgia and has remained so until now, and will be ever to come.

Folks like Helen for what it is: something out of the ordinary and easy. The ones that don't like it feel it doesn't fit their mold. Helen is its own place, catering to all kind of folks that want a little relief from the same old stuff. It's a bit like Vail on a much more common scale. For the ones that let it, Helen allows them to lose themselves in a pretend world, kind of like Disney.

That time, from July 1975 through May 1976, held more excitement than believable. It seemed like every day there was something fresh, and new folks became part of Helen daily. You would wake up excited every morning wondering what would be next. There was never a disappointing moment until May 18, 1976.

SUMMER 1975

In the Beginning

The question is always the same: "How did you ever get to Helen?" I even ask it of folks from time to time. I think it's a pretty good question, and to answer it I have to give some background in the way of a roundabout story. Because the answer is not a short one, I usually answer it in my joking manner, as I did a similar question a few weeks ago.

I was just entering Wyoming on my way to Montana when my cell phone rang. When I answered it, a friend from Helen asked me, "Where are you?" My reply caught him by surprise. Although my friends who know me well usually expect me to be anywhere but home, I think the distance away was what threw him off. Next, he asked the dreaded question, "What you doing out there?"

I gave him the kind of tongue-in-cheek answer I like the most: "Well, Jeff, Bill and I were on our way to Atlanta, but made a wrong turn. The sign I just passed said 'Welcome to Wyoming.'"

Then the next loaded question came: "Y'all going hunting?"

I thought, at the time, that the only thing I was hunting was a bathroom, but I replied, "Looking for land. There's a lot of it out here, and I haven't bought any of it yet."

I'm known to buy places most anywhere I find that I like. I've had places in Germany, Florida, South Carolina, Georgia, Alabama, and Colorado. In fact, beginning in 2003, my wife and I owned six homes. Some are rented, and some are not. Some are paid for, and some are not. It's just what I like to do. Some people have jobs; I buy homes, and that's why the folks that know me are never surprised by where I go and what I do.

So, the how-did-you-get-to-Helen question comes up quite often. The interesting thing about Helen and the surrounding area is that those of us who live here are from everywhere. People relocate from far and near. I didn't come from that far off, just down the road a piece in Atlanta, but there are people in Helen who have roots in Europe and as distant as the Far East.

My story goes like this. In the early seventies, I built a cabin on the side of Screamer Mountain out near Clayton, Georgia. While owning that, my dad and I purchased a house on Lake Burton. Both locations were within an hour's drive of Helen. One June day, I took a mountain drive and ended up there.

It was in 1975, and I was having the same trouble that more than half of America has at one point or another. My marriage was nearing an end, and it was bad! We married young and had been married for twelve years. We had two daughters under the age of ten. I tried everything I knew to make it work, but it wasn't enough. It was over, and the problem had become how to get apart. Sometimes that is harder than staying together. The bad thing for me was that I had grown up as a product of divorce, and I wanted no part of it for me or for my kids.

During the period when we were trying to reconcile, I found that if I left for a few days every now and again, it gave us both time to breathe. This is just what I did on one particular Thursday in June. I escaped the pressure by heading to the lake and on to Screamer Mountain for the weekend. On the way, I decided to go through Helen to see how their new golf course was coming along. I knew it wasn't open, but perhaps soon I'd have another place to tee up.

Meandering along the banks of the Chattahoochee River in Helen, I saw the new Helendorf Inn designed by David "Bear" Newton. Bear was one of the owners of Kingwood Country Club in Clayton at that time. Since I was a nonresident member of Kingwood, which was located on the east side of Screamer Mountain, I had a connection with this place. My membership at Kingwood? Dig this: at that point it cost me fifty dollars a year.

Back to my story: across from the Helendorf, there was a large golf green with the number-nine flag in a common pin placement. Outside the motel, there was a small sign pointing downstairs to the last room on the end that said GOLF SHOP, with another sign that said OFFICE. Looked like the place for information to me, so I pulled in the lot.

I parked, got out, and approached, hoping that I was in the right place. Three old, white, gas golf carts sat to the right. (Later, I would find out those carts came from Charlie Aaron, the father of professional golfer Tommy Aaron.) The carts, along with a single ball washer, gave some indication that I was in the right place to talk golf.

When I entered the office, there were two men and a woman talking. One man, dressed in a coat and tie, didn't seem to be in any hurry to leave. When he finally departed, I introduced myself to the couple, who were, in fact, married. They were Dick and Barbara Gay, the managers of the inn. I told them of my interest in the golf course specifically and Helen in general. I was really wasting time and trying to keep myself busy.

My interest in the Alpine village was fed by the time in the 1950s that I spent in Heidelberg, Germany, as an army dependent. Other than my daughters, it was the greatest thing to happen to me in my life. As a teenager, I played both baseball and football while there and attended an American high school named Heidelberg High with kids from all over the world. I flew over on a sixty-six-seat, four-engine prop Capital Airlines plane. It took twenty-four hours and three stops to reach Frankfurt. I would later return via a ten-day journey by ship through the English Channel and the wicked North Atlantic during the dead of winter.

I was interested in Helen. It reminded me of the place that had made such an unforgettable mark in my life some seventeen years earlier. However, the innkeepers were somewhat evasive, and giving me information didn't seem to be in their program. I'm not sure who they thought I was or what I was doing asking questions, but I was getting nowhere fast. It was a little unnerving for me to be rejected at home by my wife, and then also in Helen by strangers.

I finally asked them who could help me, and they directed me to the coat-and-tie-wearing man who had just left. They told me his name was Pete, but they couldn't tell me where I might find him at the time. I was wondering what in the hell this was all about, and why it seemed so difficult to get a straight answer. One thing was for sure, I felt the need to get out of there, because it all made little to no sense.

Even today, the events of that day don't make much sense. I got to know Dick and Barbara quite well. Now, I understand them and appreciate the years of service they have given to Helen. Barbara even went to school some time before me at Heidelberg High. Looking back, I bet they don't even remember me coming in that day in June.

The day that began a new chapter in my life continued, and for the next hour I just looked around Helen to see what had been done since my last ride through the village. It had changed since the days when we would truck our dirt bikes up from Atlanta to ride the backcountry trails of the Richard

Russell Highway. My memory flashed back to many fun times full of adventure as I drove. I passed the Wildewood Shop on a back street. It was owned and operated by some folks I had met a year earlier at the local canoe race.

A friend from Atlanta, Bill Post, and I were up here with my canoe and pop-up camper enjoying a guy's weekend on the river when we learned of the race. We checked out the details about where to camp and enter the event with the Gales, who were the owners of the local outdoor shop and sponsors of the race. We camped at the starting line, drank scotch, and cooked steaks out while preparing ourselves for the next morning's event. The Gales were from Atlanta like us, and they chucked it all to move to Helen. Bill and I were only looking for excitement, and we definitely got it.

But my reminiscing stopped there as I pulled in the parking lot to see if Anne Gale could tell me what was happening in Helen. I wanted to know if she had any information on who this masked man was that was so well protected by the folks at the Helendorf Inn. Anne remembered me from the year before and began giving me a little update on what was happening. Then, in the middle of our conversation, she stopped and said, "There's the one you need to talk to—Pete." The man in the coat and tie was going into a building across the street, which I later found out was his office.

When I headed across the street, I didn't know that this was going to be the start of a major life change. All I wanted to know was what was going on in Helen and when the golf course would be ready for play ... *my* play. I had no idea that within one week, the golf course would be mine to run! This golf course would soon change from Alpine Valley Golf Club to Bavarian Brook Golf and Racquet Club, and in the process become my dream come true.

I entered the building, as I had done about an hour

earlier at the Helendorf, introduced myself, and my new life began. Pete said he was glad I caught him, because he had just returned from a funeral. We chatted and I found him delightful to talk to, like a long-lost friend I had known forever. I'm not sure of all the details of this first conversation, but he was interested in making sure I had the answers I wanted. I felt that I could say whatever I wanted without fear of saying the wrong thing.

    I was quick to tell him more about my life than he needed to know. He had a way of setting you at ease and making you feel that you could tell him anything . . . so, I did. With my situation the way it was, I was glad to have someone to talk to. He was positive and reassuring, and he made me feel like things weren't as bad as I thought. How a complete stranger could become so comforting without judging or even really knowing me, I couldn't figure. The connection we had was instant. We were kindred spirits.

    As time passed, he would become a special mentor. What I learned from him would shape my life for years to come, as it shaped the lives of so many others. Many of the folks didn't even recognize he was influencing them, because he wasn't forceful in that way. He had a talent for leadership like no other person I've ever met.

    After our conversation, we left his office in his old Chevy station wagon full of stuff. That's the only way I can think to describe its contents: stuff. One of the many things I noticed sitting on the back seat was a couple six packs of PBR beer attached to what looked to be a parachute. I thought this a bit unusual. I remembered when as a kid, I used to make those parachutes, attach rocks, climb a tree, and let them drift to the ground. I think all kids play "war" from time to time, but I wondered what the hell Pete was doing with parachutes attached to six packs of beer. I didn't ask him that day. I reckoned it was a man's personal business what he kept in his car.

Some time later, I heard the answer to the question in a story of a friend who had entered the first Helen-to-Atlanta canoe race. Seems he and his canoeing partner were fighting the head winds, trying to cross Lake Lanier. They were just beginning to wonder why they were there, and why they had agreed to compete in a one-hundred-mile race in the first place. About then, they heard the strange sound of some kind of boat getting louder and louder. Looking in a 360-degree circle, there was nothing except water and land in view. The noise got louder and seemed to come from all around, but still no boat. Then, all of a sudden, wind and noise engulfed them like an oncoming tornado, and they saw the source of all the commotion. A plane was diving on them as if they were an enemy ship caught in the wrong place at the wrong time.

They watched in amazement as the plane banked right, turning back for another approach. This time it passed over and circled as if to take stock of the boaters and get ready for the kill. The next approach came from the left, so close that the pilot could be plainly seen when he waved and smiled. Yes, it was Pete, flying a single-engine tail-dragger plane. The racers didn't even know Pete could fly, nor did the FAA. It seems that flying lessons and a license were not part of the game for Pete. And he viewed everything as a game. He gained altitude and banked again, heading back toward the canoe. As he passed close overhead, he dropped a six pack of beer by parachute to the waiting boat.

It wasn't the only time Pete used this method to deliver beer to those in need. I know of it happening at least once more at a party on a private lake near Mount Yonah during the high-traffic period of leaf season. The story, or should I say *stories*, go on and on. Adventure was high on Pete's list of things to do. Of course, on this day in Helen, I didn't know this story as we left Pete's office on a personal tour of his little kingdom. We went on a tour of the golf course. We went through creeks, up mud banks, through roughs and fairways, and through a whole bunch of places I didn't know a Chevy station wagon could go. I saw the whole course from tees to greens. I still had no idea what was in store for me in the years to come, but Pete did. He knew I had something to contribute to his Helen puzzle. I was one of the pieces he thought he needed, and he didn't hesitate to tell me. When we returned to his office, the bait was cast. He simply said, "Why don't you become part of this madness?"

I think, at the time, his invitation went right over my head, but not for long. Less than a week later, I found myself back in Helen replying, "Okay, I'll do it!"

At the end of our time together on that evening, I bid Pete farewell, thanked him for the time, and headed to the old cabin Dad and I had purchased from my Stone Mountain neighbor on Lake Burton. Being an original 1930s lake house that had partly been redone, it had possibilities. But this night it wasn't where I needed to be, so I headed for Clayton and my cabin on Screamer Mountain.

The Screamer cabin was neat. Sitting on the north side of the mountain with a view of even more mountains to the north, it was all me. Dad and I had pieced it together from everything we'd saved and about six-thousand dollars of new material. In 1972, six-thousand dollars was a fair amount of material. It had an all-black, marble bath with a roman, six-foot, decked tub, a full kitchen that came from a burned-out home, rails from a one-hundred-year-old place we'd removed to build condos, carpet from a company we rented space to that had gone broke, and material that was purchased by mistake for the condos in Decatur that we had left over. All that added to some materials donated by suppliers whom we had worked with for years.

All in all, it was a great puzzle project. I didn't know at the time, but this would be the last weekend that I'd ever spend there. The change was beginning. I was on a path that was hidden to me, but I was taking each step as if I had known them all along.

Once I arrived at the cabin, golf at Kingwood was my first order of business. It was, after all, the whole reason I stopped by Helen in the first place: to check on if I could play golf there yet or not. Golf is never far from my thoughts. I spent the next two days golfing and enjoying the nineteenth-hole drinks of Crown Royal that had been introduced to me by an older friend named Bear. During this weekend, I got to know Bear, who was one of the new owners of Kingwood.

Bear was another interesting cat. He was an architect by trade from Gainesville, and had designed the Helendorf Inn. Coincidence? I don't think so. Everybody in the area knew Bear, and most liked him. He was a golfer who you bet against carefully, because it was easy to end a round with Bear significantly poorer than you started. I liked him.

On Saturday night, Bear invited me to dinner at the club. Handing me a coat and tie as I entered because of a new dress code, Bear offered me an opportunity. He asked me to manage his golf shop and golf course, as well as help him in real estate. He had designed new condos for Kingwood and needed help with marketing and sales. He felt it was perfect, because I needed a change and already had a place to live in the area. I agreed to meet him Sunday morning at the club to talk about it further.

Sunday, I was there from 10:00 until 11:45, before I departed. He had "no-showed" me. All I could find out was that he had a new wife, and she made him go to church with her. Disappointed, I left and headed for home in Stone Mountain.

Over the years, Bear would come and go in my life. We would play golf and sometimes do minor business together. I liked him and knew he had some problems over the course of his life. I believe it was a blessing he "no-showed" me, because shortly after he missed our meeting, he and his partners lost Kingwood for some reason. I knew him over the next twenty-five years, and not once did he ever mention the missed meeting. Bear died in 2002.

Though I was driving toward home at midday, I was not looking forward to getting there, since I knew it would be more of the same. My car turned east toward Helen. I didn't know why it did, but once I got there, guess who the first person I saw was? Yep. It was Pete, standing out in front of his office wearing a bush jacket and Scottish black beret. We spent the next three hours together talking and touring the other parts of his kingdom. This time, he showed me the vision of what he had planned for the future. The Village of Nowhere was to be an artist village only accessible by foot, carriage, or horseback. This was another of his dreams, but it would never be built. Only Pete knew his full vision, and therefore only Pete could create it, and he would have; he just didn't live long enough.

The tour went on that afternoon, and when we returned to his office, he said, "Why don't you come to Helen and run my golf course for me? What I would really like is a golf-and-tennis complex, and you are the one to do it. If you'll do it, I'll give you a piece of land of your picking on the river to build your shop. You build it, and it's all yours. I'll have all the money in the golf course, and if you agree to do this, we will work some kind of split of the money for your efforts. Also, if you will put in a small tennis center, I will lease you the land for one dollar per year for the next ten years, then the following ten years for ten percent of the gross income from the project. What do you say?"

It was too much for me to even begin to take in. My first

thought was, *What is happening this weekend with all this positive change and opportunity . . . when my personal life sucks?* It was all too good to be true. Nobody ever *gives* you anything. All I was seeking that weekend was a little mental relief and escape from rejection. Before the weekend was over, I had offers at both Kingwood and Helen! My mind was blown!

One more time, I departed. I've often wondered if Pete laughed as I headed south. He had to know the opportunity and changes it would bring were overwhelming to me. It was something I would have never considered as a possibility had it not been for his belief in the idea. It was just his way. He made the grandiose ideas seem plausible—not only plausible, but within reach. Doable. He was a dreamer who was happy to take the rest of us for a ride, and what a ride it was.

On my drive home, I took a legal pad, drawing four columns from top to bottom. The roads were not so crowded that I couldn't scribble a bit. The first two were headed KINGWOOD, one for pros and the other for cons. The third and fourth columns were the pros and cons for Helen. All the way, I kept filling in the spaces, and by the time I arrived home, Helen was the clear winner.

At this point, I thought my survey was just for fun. However, when I arrived home that Sunday and nothing had changed there, I continued to ponder my options. By Tuesday morning, I woke for the day knowing I was going to Helen. Something had happened to me, and my mind was made up. It was then that I realized that Pete's vision had become mine. The only question I had was, where did I put Pete's phone number? I searched and when I found it, I reached him on the first try. I said, "Pete, this is Hue. I've thought about it, and I'll do it. I want to come to Helen."

Pete replied, "Let me call you right back." He did, and

asked if I could be at his office by one o'clock that day. When I said yes, he added, "Bring your golf clubs."

That afternoon, Pete took me to meet Mr. J. M. Wilkins. He was the "money man" funding the dream. We played a round of golf on his private golf course, all while talking about the part I could play in the development of Helen. It was surreal for me to play a game of golf while talking of something that would be a monumental change in my life. Yet, the dreamlike state continued, and an agreement was made. Once I met Mr. Wilkins's approval, the coast was clear for me to move forward with my new life in Helen. It was up to me to follow through with promises made on that golf course that day . . . and I did.

Once we finished the golf game and went back to Pete's office, it was like I had always been part of Helen. Just making the decision had released me into this new adventure. I felt I was on a quest, and this was the beginning step of what was to become my journey. Instantly, I felt as if I belonged already. Pete asked me what I was doing the rest of the day, and I informed him that I was heading back to Atlanta. He quickly talked me into staying for dinner. Later, after offering to buy me dinner in Clarkesville, he explained the catch: he was the speaker at a Lion's Club dinner. I agreed to be his guest, and we ambled off in his old station wagon, junk and all.

The first person I recognized at the meeting was the innkeeper who'd been so unhelpful the previous Thursday at the Helendorf Inn. I mentioned it to Pete, and he quickly hauled me along toward the man. "Come on. Hue, I'd like to introduce you to Dick Gay. He and his wife manage the Helendorf." And he did. Standing face to face with him, Pete introduced us with these words: "Dick, Hue is the new manager of our golf course and will be opening a golf-and-tennis center." It was to be called "The Bavarian Brook Golf and Racquet Club."

Designer of Helen, John Kollock, celebrating with Pete Hodkinson, balloonist and one of the founders of Alpine Helen, and Hue Rainey

Photo courtesy of Jerry Brown, executive director of the Alpine Helen/White County Convention & Visitors Bureau

Helen has been known for years for its hot-air balloon race in June. In the early 1970s, Pete Hodkinson flew the Swiss Cross balloon pictured above.

Photo courtesy of Barbara Gay

He's Not Butch, He's My Brother

Not all the players in Pete's dream game were direct players; some were indirect or secondary, and some of these indirect players never even realized they were part of the game. It wasn't as if Pete didn't want to invite them in himself, it's just that they usually became involved through an unplanned manner. One of the secondary ones was my brother, Curt. I need to give you a little background so you can fully grasp how significant it was for him to become involved.

Curt grew up known as "Butchie," the preschool kid from hell. If he could get into trouble, he would. In fact, he took every chance he got to stir the pot. I feel sure the word "bad" was invented just to describe his behavior. I missed much of the bad part of his childhood, because my mother was living with my army-officer stepfather on a three-year tour in Germany from 1955 until 1958. When they left for Germany, Butchie was allowed to go with them, because he was just a baby. I was left behind, so the next time I saw him was in May of '58, when I joined them in Heidelberg for the remaining part of their tour. By this time, Butchie was four years old and running at full speed.

After a few rough years, that bad kid Butchie grew up and became known as "Butch." Later, he finished high school with all As and went on to the University of Georgia. His straight-A streak continued in journalism school, and he graduated with honors. He outgrew his nickname and changed his ways as he got older. During those college years, he decided to become who he really was: Curtis Henley Woodcock, better known as Curt. He had earned it.

I had a similar name situation. I was known as "Little Hue." The older folks that knew me growing up still call me that. My proper name is Walter Huston Rainey. I was named Walter after my grandfather and Huston for my dad. Since my dad was Hue, it stands to reason I became "Little Hue," but it never bothered me much to be named after my dad in that way. However, I never was told why they spelled my name Hue instead of Hugh, and I didn't think to ask. I have always wondered how in the world they came up with that spelling, but being as Dad is dead and Mom is not so good after a stroke, I guess it will remain a mystery. I'll just claim that I am special.

Now that you have a bit of our sibling background, I'll continue on with my story. Curt's part in Helen began after I had made the decision to move there. My dream of owning and operating a golf-and-tennis center was becoming a reality. I was anxious to share my new adventure with Mother and Curt. It was a late-summer weekend in 1975. There was a less-than-nice place called the Alpine River Lodge on the river downtown. The camper I was staying in wouldn't hold us all, so the three of us stayed at the motel together.

That night, my business was born. We talked for hours about the details. The name I had already considered for the business was the Bavarian Brook Golf and Racquet Club. We were in agreement that the name was perfect. Once that was taken care of, we all turned in for the night. During the early hours of the morning I awoke, seeing a sliver of light coming from the bathroom door. In the hall, Curt was sitting in a straight wooden chair, leaning up against the wall. The bathroom door was opened just enough to give him light to sketch with pen and paper but not wake us.

Getting up, I tiptoed back to him and whispered, "What in the world are you doing at three in the morning?"

Quickly and quietly, so as not to wake Mother up, he said, "I've got it. See if you like this!"

He had taken the name of my new operation, Bavarian Brook Golf and Racquet Club, and designed a logo that was perfect. Creating the name of the business had been easy for me. After all, the project design was to look like a Bavarian village, and it was located on the Chattahoochee River, hence Bavarian Brook . . . but I was no artist. In the wee hours of the morning, Curt had taken care of that issue for me, and he did a first-class job. The logo didn't need the first change. In two short weeks from its creation, I had the T-shirts silk-screened and printed. I was off and rolling!

Curt's support didn't end with the logo design. But he was studying broadcast journalism full time, and he worked with the UGA radio station, which was great for him, but limited his time for outside opportunities.

(As a sidenote: the Alpine River Lodge can't be found now. It was located at the end of River Street and owned and operated by a Mr. Perry. It ran down as years passed and became a cheap rental for folks working in the area. Mr. Perry was later found dead in North Carolina with hints of foul play. Alpine River Lodge was one of the first lodging businesses in Helen and had one of the better locations, being right on the bend of the river. Even without the lodge, it's still nice property.)

As I got to know Pete better, I learned that he had many ideas for Helen which he had already managed to accomplish. One was the creation of a good monthly newspaper featuring local news and produced in our small town. The paper was called the *Mountain Eagle*. It was so good that to this day, there never has been a paper in the area to match it. Many of the local business owners had monthly articles. I would write about the golf-and-racquet club. Dave Gale wrote about the outdoors, hiking, and canoeing. Many others did similar articles informing readers of all the goings-on in Helen. Folks liked the paper and couldn't wait for the next issue. However, it only lasted about a year, because it became too expensive to produce and didn't help the married life of the editor. He returned to Atlanta, we had no paper, and he still got divorced.

One more idea Pete had to help spread the word about Helen was an FM radio station. True to form, he was waiting for the right person and the right time. One day he mentioned his radio idea, and I quickly responded with what I thought might be the answer to his needs. I said, "Pete, how about Curt? He's finishing up at Georgia, where he's been working at the UGA radio station forever. He'll need a job when he's out of school."

His reply was quite a surprise, and it gave me a better understanding of his thought processes. For the first time, I could see there were limits to the game he played. He had his own set of rules that guided him through good and bad. Pete said, "Hue, it would ruin him by coming straight to Helen out of school. I know he could do it and do a good job, but it's just not the right thing for him. You see, Helen isn't real in the world we live in. The typical American doesn't think and do things like us. Helen works for us because it's pretend. People visit and like us because it's an easy way for them to pretend they're in Bavaria, but not all folks are ready to be a part of our life. To be ready, they have to be at the right place in their life.

"Curt's got to get to that place first. He doesn't need to get caught up in our make-believe village right out of college. Now, if he had been out of school working for, say, ten years, and gotten fed up with the system, Helen might be just the thing for him. He needs that time to want what we have to offer, and in turn, he would offer to us, the results being win-win for all. Let's see later what happens with Curt."

It was Pete's way. He would sum folks up and draw the good and useful talent from each. He would insert them in the game at the level he needed them and reap the benefits of success. Pete wanted his folks to be ready to play and want to win. Real team players.

Pete didn't live to check on Curt's life progress. Curt moved north for law school at Northwestern University near Chicago. Later, he went on to Portland, Oregon, where he is today with his wife and children. If I could talk to Pete, I'd tell him that I've checked on Curt. It's almost thirty years later, and he's doing what he likes and wants. Like most of us, he's found that life makes many unplanned turns, and some things don't always come the way we envision them.

It's not easy out there!

Bavarian Brook Golf Course and Racquet Club

My dad used to tell me that a person got, at most, three chances to get ahead in life—three real opportunities to get ahead and move their life forward. If you didn't respond to these offerings, they would pass you by and most likely never return. By my early thirties, I'd already passed up the chance to play professional baseball. Strike one. So, when this new chance came along, I jumped at the offer to run a golf course and racquet club in Helen.

Pete agreed to give me title to a 40 x 60–foot piece of riverfront property to build my golf-and-tennis shop, and he would also lease me another 150 x 300–foot area across from the shop to build five tennis courts. The lease terms were one dollar per year for the first ten years and 10 percent of gross income from the courts for the following ten years. My part of the deal was to run the golf course, as well as to build the shop and two tennis courts within one year. The other three courts were to come over the next four years. He was willing to give me all the income from the golf course and the shop simply for keeping the doors open. Other than seeing to that, everything was taken care of. I would have virtually no cost whatsoever.

Needless to say, I felt this was a good deal. After all, who ever heard of anyone giving away real estate, much less riverfront property? Remembering what Dad had told me, I embarked upon my adventure in Helen. As I have said previously, the deal was made over a Tuesday game of golf at Mr. Wilkins's private golf course. I picked my little spot on the river and moved in with my camper and trailer.

My father, who was my lifelong mentor, was by my side every step of the way in this new venture. He worked with me hand-in-hand to construct the golf-and-tennis shop. The little 24 x 33–foot building was built in a way no local could even imagine was possible. The back of the foundation rested in a swamp of three feet of water. Turns out it was possible, and it worked. From that small beginning, the building grew to include a full basement, a main floor for golf-and-tennis goods, a snack bar on the river with a deck, and two full-sized, top-floor apartments with lofts and decks. Seems to happen every time I build a little place, it turns out not to be so little!

The building was finished in four short months. Before the fifth month began, the shop was fully stocked, and one of the upstairs apartments was rented. I lived in the back apartment on the river. It was a nice little package and a great way to live at this point in my life. The biggest problem I had was one of the things I had hoped would get better.

My wife and I were living separately for the most part. We went to counseling once a week in Atlanta with a promise to either get together or part. We succeeded in breaking apart, and we were divorced in the fall of 1976. Living alone was a release from the previous stress of a strained marriage, but nights were rough on me. I found myself sleeping with the lights on and the radio or television going. It would take years before I was really able to handle being by myself.

It was early winter, and the building was finished and the shop was operating. My dream had come true, and I was living it. There was so much going on in Helen, with new folks coming and new happenings every day. We were on the fast track, and it looked like nothing could stop us. Everyone was excited about my little venture, either because they liked it or because they thought I'd lost my mind. Either way, I was having fun sharing it with people, and Pete had got another one trapped in his web: me.

A grand-opening celebration was in order by late winter complete with food and drink. Everybody in the area was invited, and time would show me that when there's free food and drink, every last one of them would come. It had to be one of the biggest and best parties ever thrown in Helen. My renter upstairs offered to fix the punch, which turned out to be just too good. Everyone loved it and filled their gullets to the brim with this tasty treat. By ten that night, most were drunk, and by midnight, they were laying all over the yard, putting green, and rails. We had this grand opening, but thanks to my renter, most wouldn't remember it. My dear renter had fixed the population up with a punch made of many kinds of rum that still tasted like a fruity soft drink. It's better known as "Fish House Punch." Beware if it's ever offered to you!

This could have been the beginning of the end of my little dream. But I would turn the future in another direction that kept me involved and offering what I could to the little Alpine village.

Bob Fowler, Buzz Lee, Jim Wilkins, and Pete Hodkinson

Photo by Patrick Henrickson

The original pro shop and clubhouse for the Bavarian Brook Golf Course and Racquet Club

The Bavarian Brook Racquet Club logo

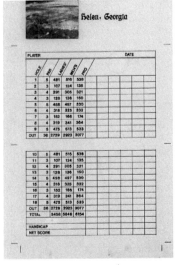

The Bavarian Brook golf course and scorecard

NOTABLES

The Good Old Boys

There are "good old boys" everywhere, in every town. In this story, there is no way to express the value of the support and help Pete had from ours. I dare say there are none like them. They were special and took pride in their roles in Pete's Helen game. Doing anything he asked of them, they would gladly jump in, because they knew he would never ask them to do anything unless he was willing to do it himself. He was special like that.

I don't have room to mention all of our good old boys, but my hat goes off to every last one of them. They know who they are, and I know for them, that is enough. They played the games for fun, not for profit. To be a part of something bigger than any one of them alone, they joined in Pete's fun.

It wasn't all fun and games. These guys had an amazing capacity for compassion and caring. If they liked you as a transplant, it meant you had earned your spot. There are some folks who have been here thirty years and still aren't considered local. Then, there are some who are instantly accepted. I was lucky enough to have been one of the latter.

Some of the men that come to mind from that era are Roy Sims, Winston Lusk, and Billy Wayne Chambers. These good old boys were always there when Pete gave a call. Roy was a successful building contractor, dirt man, sewer-and-water specialist, and whatever else he could get involved in. In fact, he was the only person who really knew where the utilities were located in Helen. If anything went wrong, the first step to fixing it was to find Roy, and he just loved that!

Pete called on Roy for the things that no one else would touch. Pete was always playing, and Roy was prone to getting a little more attention than he desired whenever Pete was at it.

As one story goes, Roy and Pete headed to the Atlanta airport to fly north to an important meeting. They had a few drinks to loosen up before boarding their flight. Once they got on the plane and took their seats, Pete told Roy he had to go to the bathroom, so he got up and headed to the front of the plane. Roy relaxed, shut his eyes, and the plane took off. When he woke up, Pete was nowhere to be found. He had gotten off the plane, leaving Roy on a flight bound for New Orleans! Pete had gotten on the correct flight and headed for his northern destination. Fun and games of another level. Pete was always at another level, and Roy was often the recipient of the set-up.

Another partner in crime was Winston, a state engineer. You see, we had two hot-air balloons and several balloon pilots that were really good at lighter-than-air flight. Winston was one of those. He also happened to be without a license to fly. The general feeling in those days was that if you had a license, you had to follow rules, and no one wanted to have rules, because rules messed with the fun. Winston could always be called on to put the balloon up and entertain the people. Obviously enjoying himself, he made you feel welcome with his Southern hospitality. The ones that seemed to enjoy visiting with him the most were the good-looking girls. He was a charmer, and he could convince a young lady into believing she could just fly off to Never, Never Land with him. The fact was, it never could have happened . . . his wife, Mary Ann, would make sure of that.

Now, on the other hand, if Pete got you in a balloon,

there was no telling where you might end up. Folks ranging from high government officials to normal tourists (if there is such a thing) have begun a harmless visit with Pete and ended up on the adventure of their life. Flying high and free was his mantra, and many of us went along for the ride.

Now, Billy Wayne was a prize! I refer to him as one of the brothers of Lanier. He was one of the most special people in the whole world. The best way to describe him is that he was always the same, and always glad to see me. It was just plain comforting. I felt honored to be accepted by Billy Wayne, because he was as local as it gets. He grew up and lived all over the area around Mount Yonah.

My first August in Helen, Dad and I were building the pro shop while Billy and his bunch were building the Hayloft Pub about 150 yards away. As the new folks in town, I'm sure they watched us as we got to work. We were working like dogs day and night, and I think it caught their eye. They didn't bother us, nor bother to introduce themselves. They just watched. I think you might call it "sizing up the city folk."

We had worked for days, and we had the main floor decked. It seemed a good time for a lunch break, so we were off to grab a bite to eat. While we were out, Habersham Hardware delivered our plywood for the next level. The heavy load was taken off the truck and stacked onto the floor. Unfortunately, it was too much weight on a place without sufficient support. It was good to have, but not where they put it.

Of course, we didn't notice the problem when we returned, so we put our nail aprons on and got back to work. Suddenly, like an explosion, the floor gave way underneath us. The temporary support broke under the heavy weight and down went the floor. Luckily for us, it was pretty well nailed together, so it only dropped about halfway into the basement. We just stood there in shock with no idea what to do next. What a mess!

After a few minutes, the realization of the fact we would basically be starting over sunk in. I was overwhelmed. Just then, I turned to see five guys led by Billy Wayne standing there, smiling. Billy said in his typical way, "You fellas having a problem?"

What happened next was my introduction to the joy and appreciation of the good old boys. Billy said to his crew, "Let's see if we can help this little situation," and they did. Dad and I just stood back and watched, amazed at their willingness and capability to get the job done. We did do one thing: we headed down and got beer for the whole group. They finished fixing our mess and we provided the beer.

As they left, Billy said, "Be careful where you put that much weight." With many thanks as well as assurances that I would pay close attention in the future, I said my goodbyes. And that was my introduction to Billy Wayne.

As I think back on it, I realize they didn't have to help us. I hate to say it, but I don't think most people would have. It's something I've come to love about mountain folks. They have this wonderful habit of helping one another, especially when one is down or in need. People moving here should take notice of that fact and thank their lucky stars that they're surrounded with so many compassionate people. I can't say enough about this endless list of good old boys and local ladies. Pete knew that building his dream would take all kinds. He was smart enough to know that different kinds of people had unique things to offer his puzzle.

Billy Wayne was one that Pete counted on to help provide Helen with much of its local color. They chased balloons, fried fish and chicken, canoed down the river, and did pretty much anything else that he asked that would draw attention to his little fantasyland. In fact, all those boys did it for the thrill of adventure. They wanted to be a part of something that Pete believed in. Whether he thanked them or not wasn't important, because they knew he would never ask anything of them he wouldn't do himself. Pete accepted and respected everyone for who they were. And besides all of that, it was fun!

From time to time I see Roy and Winston, but we all miss Billy Wayne . . . or as Lanier called him, "Brother Billy." In my case, I'd like to take this opportunity to thank those guys for helping make this my home. They showed me what compassion and caring looked like in a small town.

The Eagle Did Fly

I realize that throughout this book there will be things I have left out of the Helen story. Anyone who was a part of Helen at this time has his or her own special memories. I only wish I could remember everything. However, it has been over thirty years, and memories fade into the mist after so many years. Of all of us who walked this path together, there is one thing we should not forget: our local newspaper.

The *Mountain Eagle* was far ahead of its time, and still to this day is the best newspaper we've ever had. It was a professional paper, especially for such a small town, and you can't beat that name. Phil Garner and Larry Woods, both from the Atlanta news world, were behind it. Both lived and worked in Atlanta during what I call the "growing-pain days," when Atlanta was growing from a good-sized city to becoming a large professional city. Like all of us that had migrated to Helen, Larry and Phil found stress relief and fun in Pete's world, and like the rest of us, they became part of his puzzle. Both men were outgoing figures and loved the free-spirited excitement that came with being a part of Helen.

When they came on to the scene, they provided Pete with a vehicle to get the word out with very little expense. Once he had talked to them for about ten minutes, he had his tools. Getting to know them resulted in a monthly paper. I say monthly, but it seemed it would appear whenever there was good news. The paper was human-interest driven, and generally told what had happened or what was going to happen in the area. Phil had all of us writing about what we were up to and what we were going to do, from tennis to canoeing all the way to Dig Mo, a local septic-tank company.

If you could read a copy, you would understand the ability of the paper to capture the energy of the times. Being employed by network television, Larry could do his part rather easy. On the other hand, Phil had to be careful because of his *Atlanta Journal* employment. They were not too keen on one of their writers contributing to other publications, but he managed.

There was one particularly active young man in Helen whose camera provided all the pictures the *Mountain Eagle* would need. Pat Henrickson was another gift to the area. Long after Phil and Larry were gone, Pat carried forward with the paper until a lack of funds would not allow him to do his work. One note of interest is that while Pete got his paper (and a good one at that), he never got the FM radio station he wanted so badly. How much could one man do in ten short months? With help from friends, more than most. There were many of us who contributed, never even considering making money for our efforts. We did it so that others could succeed and fulfill their dreams. Call it a team effort, call it collaboration, call it whatever you want . . . we called it fun!

FALL 1975

Pete's Nowhere?
It's Nowhere to Be Found

Just a couple days before I decided to come to Helen, Pete was showing me the bluff overlooking the Chattahoochee River where a new villa project would one day be perched. The project was going to be made up of buildings consisting of between four and six circular units, with a courtyard and tennis court for each grouping. He hadn't yet decided whether each group of villas should also have its own clubhouse and pool, or whether one would be enough for the entire project. These tennis villas were going to be located on the river side of the old Unicoi rail line. That was just past the number-five fairway, a dog-leg right par five of the then Alpine Valley Golf Course, which was later to be known as the Bavarian Brook Golf and Racquet Club.

(Sidenote: If you're trying to figure out this dream-villa location, find the Wilder Forest Condos, and you've got it. They were built in the early 1980s after Pete was long gone. They look like what the developers and investors planned, not what Pete had envisioned exactly. Despite that, they turned out pretty good and have been a stepping stone to other development in Helen. Wilder Forest is just one of many seeds Pete planted for others to cultivate. It was his way to plant the seed of an idea for someone else to carry out.)

On this day, as we were walking the bluff discussing his villa project, I first heard Pete mention his dream village of "Nowhere." Pete was showing me around the bluff when we saw a man on a horse making his way up the old rail line. At one time, that route was used to bring timber from Unicoi State Park to the Helen mill for processing. As we watched, the horse and rider disappeared into the forest along a cool mountain stream named Belle Branch.

I asked Pete, "Where's he going?"

Pete's reply was simple: "Nowhere."

"Come on, Pete. He's going somewhere!" I replied.

Pete agreed, "That's just it, he's heading to Nowhere. He just doesn't know it."

Pete knew I didn't have a clue what he was talking about. He began to explain his vision of Nowhere. He told me that when the timing was right, maybe when Helen needed a shot of something new to excite the tourists, he would develop the village of Nowhere.

The concept was quite interesting. Just past the bluff where we were standing, the old Unicoi railbed would become an improved route winding over a mile to an international art village called Nowhere. There would be several ways of getting there (foot, horseback, carriage, or bike), but none of those would include any means of motor travel.

As for the artists, they would set up in rustic huts that they could rent for either weekends or for the season. They would get their goods to Nowhere the same way as everyone else. It would have been kind of like Cherokee's "Indian Village" without the Indians. What a wonderful idea!

It never happened, because no one ever really knew of Pete's idea. Built of rough lumber with no electric service and paths of sawdust and gravel, Nowhere might have been one of the greatest and cheapest ideas yet. Folks would have loved this mountain novelty. I can see the promotion now: "When you got nowhere to go, go to Nowhere." There are a thousand ways to play with that name for marketing purposes. It would have been a fun adventure, to be sure. But in the end, it went . . . nowhere.

As it was, Pete always stayed several steps ahead with his dreams, and it seemed that one dream led to another. He was such a talent and one that has not received due recognition.

Chamber of Commerce

Once upon a time in the little Northeast Georgia village of Helen, there lived a king named Pete. He was a good and just king with many villagers whose welfare he protected. In turn, they helped build the kingdom by contributing the many little things that they had to offer. By working together, the little village became stronger and stronger until it was known far and wide as a Georgia destination not to be missed.

King Pete saw that his village was growing into a tourist center. He realized it needed direction to continue building its appeal throughout the land. So, the king pushed for the formation of a local chamber of commerce. After all, most of the other successful villages had one. The chamber was formed and saw villagers and those from the surrounding area all join together, and it was good.

Now, like most gatherings of varied kinds of folk, everybody in the chamber had their own ideas on how things should be run. And also, like most gatherings of varied kinds of folk, there were some there whose egos demanded they speak simply to hear themselves speak. This is how I found the Helen chamber meeting on my first visit as a new resident and business owner in Helen.

Having met Dave and Anne Gale before signing on to be a part of Pete's village, Dave asked me to attend the monthly chamber meeting with him. He was on the board and wanted to introduce me to some of the key players in Helen. So, on that hot summer night, we made our way to the meeting at Das Apple Haus Restaurant. We arrived to a full house with plenty to eat and drink. I learned one lesson about Helen's business community that night: never give them something to drink before the business is done. The group was well-lubricated as the meeting began, and in a short time, things were completely out of order. Folks were shouting, carrying on, and looked as though they were going to fight. Dave got so mad that he stormed out and there I was, knowing no one and left alone in a group of mad villagers.

I was not missed when I departed as soon as I could afterward. I would like to tell you things have gotten better over the years, but I can't. Almost thirty years later, and all hell can still break loose at a Helen Chamber of Commerce meeting. Although the threat of fighting has diminished as they've gotten older, some of the same players are still involved.

Pete laughed when I spoke with him about the chamber a little later. He asked if I noticed that he wasn't there. I had noticed, and I asked, "But didn't you help get it started?"

"Yeah," he replied, "I did, and I support it, but I don't get personally involved on a regular basis." He then added a little advice, saying, "Always ask the chamber to cosponsor anything you do or want to do that involves an event or bringing folks to the area. Tell them you or your folks will put the event on, and that you would like them to advertise and help get the word out. They'll love it. They love getting the credit without having to do the work. Anyhow, if they did the work, it would mean they have to get everything organized, and that's not going to happen without a fight, like you saw last night. That's how you win with the chamber. Your event is successful because you did it like you wanted and they get credit, which helps us all."

He was right, and his is the approach I take to this day.

It works. My first real try with the chamber was for a bike race I held in the spring of 1976. Putting Pete's advice into action, the event was a hit. However, the real measure of success was that it received primetime coverage on two of Atlanta's three network-news programs.

Later in the year, in November, Helen was named number one in the professional tourism category by Stay and See America in Georgia. Can you believe a brand-new little village made up of folks from everywhere could become number one in the state in such a short time? Take me, for instance. Just six months earlier I was a floundering defunct contractor from Atlanta with a marriage that was shot. At that time, I didn't even have a clue what Helen was all about, nor did I care. Now here I was, embarking on a new journey and caught up with the momentum of the dream. It was surreal, but on the night of December 2, 1975, Mayor Bob Fowler, King Pete Hodkinson, outfitter and wilderness guide Dave Gale, business and chamber leader Buzz Lee, and I accepted the award from former Governor Carl E. Sanders. We accepted it at the Stay and See America in Georgia awards banquet at the Hyatt Regency in Atlanta.

The amazing thing was that all the great and wonderful places in Georgia were who we were competing with. Truth be known, we didn't have a professional tourism organization, and we had very little money with which to operate, but we had the important things. We had heart and a free spirit, which filtered down from Pete. We might have been stubborn about things in some ways, but we cared about one another and the town's success. We cared about Helen and what we were doing. It made complete sense to us, and we endured to make our mark in Georgia. "Failure" and "quit" weren't words in our vocabulary.

The judges called Helen "an outstanding success story that's almost unbelievable. The town has a high concentration of people who not only have drive, but talent, ingenuity, and openness to the possibilities around them. Helen is an outstanding example for every small town in the nation, proving that when a few people put their minds to it, they can perform what seems like a miracle."*

What a great description of our crew, and we had Pete to thank for it. He had led us to be an award-winning group. We went on to win more awards and continued to shine as a tourist destination. People now visit Helen from all over Georgia and the rest of the United States. We even get a good number of international visitors each year.

Twelve percent of Helen's population went to Atlanta to accept Helen's award as winner of the Stay and See America in Georgia professional category. Pictured above at the banquet are then–Helen Mayor Bob Fowler, Peter Hodkinson, Buzz Lee, Jimmy Gonia, Dave Gale, and Hue Rainey.

Photo by John Kollock

---

* "Town Leaders Accept Stay, See Award." *The Times* (Gainesville, GA), December 3, 1975.

The Secrets of Hilltop House

Learning about Pete came quick after my move to Helen, and as each week passed, I learned ever so much more. He was different from anyone I had ever come in contact with because of his power to draw attention to whatever he chose. He also had mastered the art of deception, which I would learn to appreciate one late-summer Saturday afternoon.

On this day with tourists everywhere, Pete was on a mission. You could just tell when he was up to something by looking at him. He would start gathering folks, and the plot would thicken. At his request, several of the good old boys had gathered at his office with their pickup trucks. I didn't want to be left out. I was the new guy in town, after all, so I went, even though I had no clue what was next. I figured it was a good way to get to know the locals, and one couldn't know enough locals.

Pete greeted me with glee, saying, "Hue, I'm glad you're here! I need some help, and you've got just the right auto for the job—your three-quarter-ton pickup truck. How about it?"

With that, I joined the good old boys, and we all followed Pete out of the parking lot and across the river bridge. Then, we went right through Paul's Steakhouse parking lot and up a dirt road that I didn't even know was there. Up the road, we took a left into a driveway with a small sign lettered with the words HILLTOP HOUSE. It was far from the top of the hill, but I'm sure it was high enough for someone to give it the title.

Pete had sold this Hilltop House to an older couple from

the other side of North Georgia, and he had to get all his stuff out. Time was running out. In other words, we were the movers. He gave everyone their instructions, except me. Off they went, like it was an everyday happening. Then, turning to me, Pete said, "How about helping me with this storage building? Your truck is just right for the job."

I backed up to the door as he opened it. I couldn't believe my eyes. The building was full of cases that contained gallons of relish and pickles. I knew more about these items than Pete did. See, I grew up in the wholesale grocery business and had loaded more trucks for delivery with these same products than Pete would have ever believed.

"Pete, what the hell you doing with all this stuff, and what you going to do with it?"

He said he was going to take it to the dump, which was a real shock to me, since I knew how much the stuff cost. All of it was expensive, and all of it was still good. Now, anyone who knows me knows what I did. Yep, I kept it, and it later ended up at my and my dad's place at Lake Burton, where we enjoyed it for years to come. I don't throw away much. Pete gave me his blessing to keep the stuff, even though he thought I was crazy.

Later on, he told me why he had such a stock of goods. When the main part of the village was redone, he had a couple shops that stood empty. "It just didn't look good," he said. "So, I got me a couple little old ladies, dressed them up in a country bonnet, and opened a country store with fresh, garden-grown canned relish and pickles. My little ladies would work in the back of the shop filling the pint canning jars with the commercial relish and pickles. Then they made handwritten labels stating what it was and whose garden it came from. I had a pretty good business, and the tourists loved it."

"Pete, that doesn't sound quite right. What happened?"

He answered, "What happened was, someone came along and wanted shop space. I sold the shop, and all was good. But that wasn't the only shop I did that way," he told me. "There was a quilt shop that I had a little lady run who would quilt on site. I sold a lot of factory quilts there until I moved that shop. No one got hurt. We all won."

I had learned more about Pete and how he got his vision accomplished all while loading my truck up with pickles.

Turning to the other side of the little storage building, he said, "Give me a hand with this. It's something I want you to have." I helped him pick up a large 1917 National Crank cash register and put it in my truck. "Hue, I want you to have this to keep all the money you're going to make in Helen."

I thanked him for the relish, pickles, and cash register. Off I went. What a day, and my understanding of Pete was just beginning. There would be many more days like this summer Saturday, and many more learning experiences with Pete. We crammed a lot in ten short months. Wonder what it would have been like if there had been more time. That was 1975, and this is 2019, and I've still got my cash register.

Dreams and Corporations

It was Pete's way of getting things done. He had an idea that met a need, and first thing he did was form a corporation with local stock offerings. He was sure to get a checkbook to make it official, but he didn't buy a lot of blank checks, because they most likely wouldn't be needed.

This is how he handled three corporations that came to his mind during the fall of '75 and winter of '76. They were the Alpine Valley Transit Authority, Helen Ice Corporation, and Theater Helen, Inc. I had stock in the latter two, but I didn't buy it. No one did.

Alpine Valley Transit was going to be a way to transport folks around the city. He had a trolley built to run on a track. It never got much beyond the trolley. Helen Ice, the corporation to provide an ice rink for skating, never got any further than the stock issue. In fact, its water never got frozen, although the ponds on the golf course froze during the hard winter.

Downtown Helen already had a local theater production of *The Sound of Music*, which played nightly to full-house crowds. It even turned people away from time to time. This was mainly due to the limited seating of ninety in the little theater. A new and larger playhouse was needed for this proven production.

Theater Helen, Inc. was formed and stock was offered for sale. Support came easily, because it was already successful and local supporters like the arts. Pete cut some choice property out of the Valley located only one hundred yards from the Helendorf Inn and Highway 75, easily seen by all.

53

A theater group that wanted to provide the production did a design. In other words, a little trading was taking place. Trading didn't stop there. Pete had approached local building-material supply companies that offered to donate material for construction. Who said you needed money?

Now, all he needed was someone to look out for the construction. I was appointed. It was a no-pay job. I could have gotten stock at a later date for my efforts if things went well. I didn't care; just being a part of the program was enough for me. It was to be a three-hundred-seat theater with all the bells and whistles. The floor was poured concrete, and three of the outside walls were blocked up. The stage was built and had a professional 360-degree stage turntable installed for easy set changing. It was on the way to reality. We had a great bunch at that time all working together.

When Pete died, so did the theater. It was only as strong as its leader. No one could or would take it forward. The high winds came and freezing weather weakened the walls, making them dangerous. The decision was made to have the walls pushed down, which left a pile of rubble. Another memorial to Pete.

Some years later, there was talk of danger with a pile of rubble of that size just sitting there. Being the civic-minded person I was, I took my truck and hand tools, and removed every bit of the stage and turntable. I used all of the 2 x 10s and 2 x 12s, along with three-quarter-inch plywood, to add several more motel rooms on my Bavarian Brook Lodge.

The theater building, like so many other things, went with Pete. Some years later, theater was tried in the Festhalle, but it just wasn't the right space for it. It finally found a home at the Sautee Nacoochee Community Center, which still holds productions today.

Early-Morning Return

It was around six thirty on a Monday morning when I rounded the curves entering Helen. It had been another long weekend at home in Stone Mountain with my family, and I was returning for several days to my new adventure in Helen. That's how I approached the change in my life: three or four days at home and three or four days in Helen. I look at it much the same way I did when I traveled selling sewing notions for a company in Atlanta. I would head to South Georgia on Mondays, returning on Thursday or Friday. It was the way I justified being away from my girls.

As the road straightened out, passing the Station Inn on the left, I noticed Pete's station wagon parked on the right shoulder with his tailgate down. He was sitting there dressed in jeans, a blue golf shirt, lightweight bush jacket, and tan, suede shoes. He was looking across his Alpine valley. It was covered with golf courses and an area he called "the island."

The island had begun with the construction of the Hayloft Pub and another massive building to be called Lo Lu's. The pub was nearing completion, while work on Lo Lu's was just beginning. The only other thing happening in the area was my building on the river. It would serve as my golf/tennis pro shop and grill, with two small apartments upstairs. I would live in one of them, and the other would be a rental. My first two tennis courts were also under construction.

I slowed and stopped just beyond Pete, parked, and

made my way to the rear of his car. "Pete, what you doing at this time of the morning?"

He replied, "I've got it all figured out."

"What figured out?" I asked.

He pointed to the area of the ninth fairway, a long par five that would be a spot for landing a really good drive, and said, "That will be known as the Canal Area or Canal Shops."

It was an area that wouldn't drain because it was fed by springs, and it looked like a natural lake. It was the kind of land that was best used as a water hazard on number nine. But in Pete's eyes, it was something altogether different. He reached behind him and pulled out several legal pads, on which he'd formed this creative new concept that morning. The area would branch off the moat that surrounded the island area. It was laid out in a winding mass of 40 x 60 and 60 x 60 lots, making up a complete village like you find throughout Bavaria. He had already sold most of the island area to hopeful investors at five thousand dollars to ten thousand dollars per plot. Now he was thinking, *Why stop now? The more the better!* All he had to do was create a plan, have it put to paper as a rendering, and then he was ready to market.

Pete knew he could sell a certain number of canal lots on concept alone, creating enough money to have the area surveyed so he could really market the rest. By the time he got the concept sold, folks would be standing in line for the remaining spots. Of course, Pete always had his fronts, who were folks like me that would agree to be a so-called investor helping his cause. There were many of us, and we knew if we played the game with Pete, it would come back to us along the way.

I asked Pete what would happen to our ninth hole. I

told him we couldn't have an eight-hole golf course. He jokingly said, "Why not? We were listed in the State of Georgia Tourism information as having a one-hole golf course. Why not go for eight? We've got them." Then, he got more serious and explained how we could make changes to number nine and the course would be better for it. I never dreamed today there would be little hint of that initial golf course in the Helen Alpine valley. I can point out the remains of old tee boxes and greens, but without the few of us who know, there is no way of guessing it was ever there.

As for the canal area and its shops, it never had the first shovel of dirt moved, although Pete did have two real investors put money up based on the concept. I'm sure they just had to be first. And they were—first and last. Somehow, they did get their money back after Pete's death.

What a web he did spin, and my, how he could trap the unexpected. If you were greedy and didn't play the game, chances were good you would end up with worthless real estate or just plain be relieved of your money. If you played and bet on the game, the chances looked much brighter.

I left Pete sitting there dreaming of his kingdom and the players he could include. The interesting thing is, his dreams had nothing to do with him making money. It was more of what he could make, or create next, and how he could do it. I'm not sure he ever thought of what was in it for him; he just enjoyed the feeling of success. At the rate he went, it was as if he was racing against time.

Could he have known something we didn't?

Where Did You Say the Chattahoochee Started?

My dear tennis partner, Charles, was anything but normal. We all figured it was because he grew up in South Florida and came from a wealthier family. He was a real estate broker and lived with his wife at Lake Burton.

I met Charles soon after making the Helen move, and he quickly became a regular at Bavarian Brook Golf and Racquet Club. In fact, he rented the upstairs valley-view apartment above my shop. I lived in the one to the rear on the river. Much of our time in the midseventies was spent playing as part of our work. That was the great thing about Pete's Helen. In those days, our work was our play, and our play was our work. What a wonderful little world we lived in. Seems like the more we played, the better we did. I guess it was because our play mostly was directed at creating publicity for the cause . . . the Helen cause, that is.

Charles and I teamed up as double partners every time there was a taker, and most of the time, we would win. I have to disclose that it wasn't because of my ability, but rather his. He was about the best around. His serve was unreturnable and the rest of his game dominated our opponents. Once we graced the court, we had an understanding. He would always have me play up at the net and watch the alley. He never wanted me to the back. I didn't really like this, but soon I found out his reasoning. First, he felt he was good enough to beat any two players if the court was reduced to a singles court on our side. If I was covering three feet to the alley side and three feet to the open-court side, all that was left was a single-size court for him to work. He did just that!

The other thing he wanted from me was a quick point at the net, which I could do quite well if I didn't have to move around too much. That all worked and I stayed out of his way. That was of utmost importance.

Now, he may have been the best at tennis, but we all would clean his clock on the links. Golf just wasn't his cup of tea, but he tried and developed a right fair game. It's always been said that to get better at golf, you've got to play, and play we did—all the time.

As I mentioned, Charles was one of the first folks Pete introduced me to in Helen. It was a natural introduction because of Charles's love for tennis. I will never forget how he responded to Pete's introduction to the new kid on the block. He didn't say "Glad to meet you" or "Glad you are going to do what you're going to do." Rather, he said something like this: "That's something I had planned to do, but I've been tied up with other real estate projects."

Guess I beat him to it. Maybe that's why he beat me all over the court when we had our daily set. With all that said, there was another side to Charles. He was a hell of a lot of fun. Whether we were playing tennis, golf, partying, or planning some adventure, it was fun to have Charles as part of it.

One thing he did differently than most was drink rum and Tab. Rarely would anyone see Charles when he didn't have a Tab close at hand. Where he had Tab, he had rum, which was his drink of choice. Bet he still drinks rum and something today. There are many Charles stories during this time frame, but the one that is dearest to me is our wilderness hike in late November to find the main spring that starts the Chattahoochee River.

This was another publicity stunt dreamed up by a conversation between Pete and Phil Garner of the Atlanta paper. Phil was an active player in Helen. Starting way before its time was a great little newspaper of local news called the *Mountain Eagle*. There never was or has been a newspaper in this area that could hold a light to the *Mountain Eagle*. It was unfortunate the *Mountain Eagle* had a short life of less than a year. In this endeavor, Phil was helped by fellow journalist Larry Woods of Atlanta TV news. You could catch Larry on TV about any day or night doing his special reports. His ability to know important people was like gold to Phil. Together, they spun local stories and happy happenings in the Helen area, something unheard of in news. Have you ever seen or heard much happy news? Doesn't seem to be the American way. Folks just like to hear the crap, and it sells. Too bad for us!

Anyhow, Pete and Phil decided the Atlanta magazine section of the Sunday paper, which covered the South like the dew, needed a great story about a local group of adventurers setting out on foot with full camping gear to discover the daddy spring that begins the famous Chattahoochee River, which travels from near the Appalachian Trail north of Helen to the Gulf of Mexico. Of course, it does more than just flow from point to point. It provides water for towns along the way, including Atlanta, and lakes such as Lake Lanier near Gainesville and Lake George to the south. It also forms a division in places of Georgia and Alabama.

Who would do this great adventure? Pete picked the ones he could get the most mileage from. He wanted people that folks in other areas would notice by name. Dave Gale, owner/operator of the Wildewood Shop, was picked to lead, not only because of his having the only outfitting shop in the area, but also for the fact he had chucked it all and moved from Atlanta, leaving his engineering-and-construction business. He was a very visible fellow.

I was next, due to being a sportsman and also for leaving Atlanta to seek a dream of having my own golf-and-tennis center. I was well known from my Atlanta sports success, and the Rainey family had made its mark on basketball-and-baseball history throughout Georgia. There would be a good chance that readers would know the Rainey name in print and gain interest.

Then came Warren and Jimmy Smyth from the South Florida area. Warren was owner/operator of the Strudel Haus restaurant in Helen, known for its class, good food, and the blue roof. Jimmy was his son, who took an active part of his father's business. Warren had been director of the Miami Chamber of Commerce and was well known in the South Florida area. Jimmy was also very much liked, so they were naturals for the adventure.

Then came Charles, who didn't want to miss out on the fun. Pete and I talked about Charles being one of the chosen few and decided he could add color to an already colorful bunch. He was from a well-known Miami family, and his name in print was sure to be noticed.

Why the folks from Miami? It seems that Phil had figured out how the same human-interest story could be placed in the Miami paper, which covered Florida like the waves. So, the South would be well covered. It was all in the name of fun and didn't cost a dime. What an idea! Wonder who dreamed it up? Pete comes to mind.

The sixth adventurer of the group was the local transplanted photographer from Atlanta, Patrick Henrickson. He was a last-minute addition. This was Phil's idea because of the need for photos of the discovery. Pat was fun and a good sportsman. He fit right in.

The big day came, and we all met at Pete's office early in the morning with all our gear ready. We had three tents, and we knew who our tent mate would be. Mine was Charles. We also knew that it would be two days and one night in the mountains in freezing weather. It was not a problem to a group like this. Pete got us together for farewell drinks, then loaded us into a truck. We headed for the head of the river in the national forest. Off we went, packs and all, with Pete and his assistant following in his Chevy station wagon.

At the beginning point, we unloaded and mounted our gear with stocking caps covering our heads. As Pete bid us a successful trip and while pictures were being taken, he came up from behind and asked if I had any room in my pack. With my positive reply, he inserted a package in the left side. Of course, I couldn't see to the rear, but I knew my load had been increased. Off we went like puppy dogs following a mama dog. The adventure was underway.

That day we hiked slowly uphill following the largest supplying branch of water. Every time the creek would fork off, we would go with the larger branch. When in doubt of which one was larger, we would split up until one was proven to be dormant. That day we found two of the neatest waterfalls, the first being filled with a heavy volume of water and the second being very high, falling from a cliff above. After traversing the cliff, we reached the top and found patches of snow.

Late in the afternoon, we decided above the falls was a good spot for camp. It would leave us an easy next-day hike to find the main spring, intersect the trail, and hike the five miles or so out to Highway 75. Charles and I pitched our tent and made ready for the dark to come. We gathered firewood and got a nice fire going for warmth, which was a joke. The only place warm was our sleeping bags. If you've ever done something like this, you know that there isn't much to do after dark. A good, warm sleeping bag is gold and becomes your home for the evening.

As for Charles and me, we had a wonderful advantage on the others. It turned out to be a camp of "tent fun" and "tent boring." Thanks to Pete and his inserted package in my pack, we were the only tent fun, as far as we knew. The package turned out to be a quart of J&B Scotch, a good drink with the little water we had.

We had made sure our tent was a ways from the others, so we wouldn't be a bother. After a good camp meal together, we retired for our well-kept secret: a nightcap. What I can tell you is that it was more than a nightcap, because carrying a half-filled bottle out of the wilderness wasn't in either of our plans. The scotch itself had a strange taste, but after a couple drinks, we didn't care what it tasted like; it was all we had. The next day we broke camp and found the main feeder spring some one hundred feet south of the trail. It was much bigger than I would have thought, and the water volume flowed freely.

There's a little more to this tale. The newspaper story did what it was supposed to, as it was being read throughout the South. Once again, Pete had pulled off free publicity, and Helen was becoming known in the Southeast. It was always part of his plan: Just get them here, and they will spend money. They might even become a part of a dream deep within.

As for the scotch, it wasn't all scotch. It seems Pete had part of a bottle of J&B, as well as other drinks of choice. In his time of need, he became a chemist mixing his stock to make a new type of scotch: Pete's scotch.

NOTABLES

Chief

Being located smack dab in the middle of the Cherokee and Creek Indian historical area, Helen has blessed us with an ongoing Native American heritage that is visible everywhere! There are stores that sell all types of Native American items, not to mention all the folks prowling around hunting for arrowheads and pottery scattered throughout the Valley. Protestors stand against anything being built on possible Native American historical sites. The influence is noticeable around town, and it is also in the stories passed down for generations.

For example, the Sautee-Nacoochee Valley draws its name from the legend of a pair of lovers from rival tribes. You can find that story written by many local writers, and I highly recommend that you take the time to read at least one of the fictional versions that can be found around town for the color it brings.

Among the stories is one of a man known as Chief. However, his title is misleading. I don't know that much about his heritage, other than that his family was an old-time local mountain family. I do know he wasn't a real Native American chief, which seems odd here in the heart of Cherokee and Creek land. His nickname was "Chief," and that's all that folks called him. It was a fact that everyone knew and liked him. He had an auto mechanic shop that was wedged in between several other locally owned businesses.

On one side, there was the famous Mynah Bird Restaurant, where people could enjoy all the Vietnamese cuisine they could eat and choose from a large variety of imported gifts and novelties. The Mynah Bird was a special place. It was unique in that it was the only authentic Vietnamese restaurant in the South, right in the middle of Helen. Pete never missed a chance to show it off. Any time he had someone he was trying to impress, they went to the Mynah Bird. He also made sure the Atlanta papers and media were aware of our special Mynah Bird eating spot.

It's no secret that the restaurant business is tough with very little reward, and it was no different with the Mynah Bird. I can't count the number of times Pete would get twelve to twenty of us together for free drinks at his office in the late afternoon. It was social fun for all and got everyone a little loose before he would suggest we go, as a group, to one of the ailing restaurants for dinner. It would just about always be the Mynah Bird or the Sautee Inn in the Valley. We had to eat somewhere, and the Chicken Tree at the Sautee Inn was a novelty. Whoever heard of a tree full of chickens next to the entrance of a restaurant? I know where their chicken dishes came from!

Both restaurants always needed business, and both were important in Pete's plan of success. He wanted to keep them afloat, and an occasional party of twenty went a little way to helping that cause. The owner of the Mynah Bird was a well-educated young lady from Vietnam who later closed her restaurant and took a position with the federal government in Washington. Sometime after that, the restaurant was closed and the space sold for a gift shop.

On the other side of Chief's shop was the Haus of Tyrol. It was owned by an Austrian photographer who came to town to take pretty pictures of a North Georgia mountain village. He wanted to capture it on film, because it looked like his childhood home near Innsbruck, Austria. He and his wife liked what they saw so much, they made the move from Atlanta to open an Austrian gift store that sold only imports. It soon became one of the largest mail-order import businesses of its kind.

See, they just came from everywhere. They saw an opportunity and stayed to become part of the ongoing game. Some made it and some didn't, but Haus of Tyrol made it big.

Chief had many other neighbors, including a drugstore that sold more ice cream than drugs, and a Christian bookstore. All were equally important to the overall plan. However, Chief was the only auto mechanic in our little area. His shop was right on Main Street and had been for as long as anyone could remember. It was newly Alpine, like all the other buildings in the city strip. The transformation of the Downtown area was something to behold. There are before-and-after photos in some of the books of the history of Helen. Chief was an unlikely player in Pete's game, but he was as much a part of it as any of us.

His shop was something to take in. Early in the morning, he would roll up his door and open his world for all to see. It was like another realm in there. Stuff was everywhere, and the floor was coated with several inches of grease and oil. He had parts and tools on every surface—not organized on tables and racks, but I mean all over the place. Like most old-timers, he knew where everything was, and if it wasn't a problem to him, it wasn't a problem at all. In the evening, he would roll down the door and all looked like the perfect little Alpine building.

Chief was a little man, always in overalls and a kind of mechanic's railroad cloth cap. I bet he didn't weigh 145 pounds when wet, but every pound of him was good. In fact, he rates right at the top of my list of all-time good folks. He was a damn good mechanic to boot. You know, the kind who fixes things rather than replacing them. He could fix just about anything, and if he couldn't fix it, he would rebuild it.

The story goes that when he was young, this little mountain mechanic was featured in *Popular Mechanics* magazine for something he had invented. So, everyone around knew that if you needed your car, motorbike, or even lawnmower fixed, Chief was the man to see. It might take standing around his shop for a while, but sooner or later you would get the chance to ask for help, and you would get it.

After he fixed your problem machine, you would ask the question, "Chief, how much do I owe you?"

Most likely his reply would be, "Is six bucks too much?"

I can remember thinking, *Hell no, it isn't too much! It should be much more.* But I never said it that way, not to Chief. I did ask him if he was sure and told him it should be more, but he would never up his price.

Where have all the Chiefs gone?

Pete always thought highly of Chief and knew how much he meant to the area. Chief was not just a locally colorful character, but also a damn good mechanic who was well known. He was a good man and fit well into Pete's collection of special offerings in Helen. Helen was special because of these unique folks that made it up, and Pete knew it.

Chief outlived Pete and was grieved by Pete's passing, as we all were. It would be truer to say we all were lost and unsure of our future. However, Chief knew where he fit, and he went on doing just what he had always done. He continued fixing things until one morning his heart quit right there under a car in his shop, doing his thing. I'm sure the price for whatever he was fixing would have been six dollars.

Chief was one of those folks who cannot be replaced. He was a product of better times. Nowadays, Helen folks have no idea of the Chiefs and Petes, as well as the others who made up those beginning years. In the place where his garage used to be, there's now a shopping mall filled with stuff that can't be bought for anywhere near six dollars, and surely wasn't made or fixed on site.

Chief's Garage, like the Mynah Bird and the Sautee Inn, played a part in Pete's game of building a tourism giant in Georgia, and helped give future players a chance to try to succeed. I wonder, if they knew about the people who came before them, would they try a little harder now? Would the newer people to Helen join the community game, or just do business here for themselves?

There were many of these early businesses that laid the groundwork for others to come. Where have they all gone? They did the hard work, but you can bet, looking back, they had the joy and excitement of being the first of their kind. Like true free spirits, they fulfilled a dream made possible by their leader, the dreamer, Pete.

Chief Westmoreland's garage located in Downtown Helen and pictures of him working in and around his garage

Photos courtesy of Chief Westmoreland's family

Sharing His Candy

There have probably been thousands of individuals who've earned at least some share of credit in the success of Helen. I don't have space to mention all of them, but I have no doubt they know who they are. They've all been players in Pete's game, whether their role ended in disappointment or reward.

One of these players is special, not only because we're friends and our history together in Helen goes way back, but because he is still playing the game after thirty years. And I might say he plays it very, very successfully. He's David Jones, better known as "the candy man."

David came to Helen from Atlanta about two years before my arrival. He, like many of us, was looking for a new life in a new place and, totally by chance, found the ultimate provider, Pete. Of course, Pete had empty spots in his puzzle and a specific place for David, so he was easily plugged in. David and his wife, Janet, were the first lodge-keepers of the new Alpine lodging property, the Helendorf Inn. This property was located on the banks of the Chattahoochee River in Downtown Helen.

Being lodge-keepers, they didn't only rent the rooms; they also cleaned them. They did their own landscaping, too. In those days in Helen, a person would do everything themselves. In fact, they even cooked steak dinners for their guests. This dining event took place in the lodge office on the other side of the street in the Downtown area.

This office would later serve as Pete's office and the physical address of many active and inactive corporations born out of Pete's imagination. The main one was the Alpine Valley Investment Corp. It was the controlling entity for most of Pete's development games.

For some reason, Pete decided to rearrange David's little puzzle piece and plug it into a different space. So, David became the owner and operator of a small candy store. It was set up in a tiny empty space of under four hundred square feet on Old Street, the most charming shopping area in Helen. The paintings on the buildings of Old Street were some of John Kollock's finest work and have been photographed by people from all over the world.

Presented with the opportunity to have his own candy store, David had one small concern. "I know nothing about candy," he told Pete.

Pete responded confidently, "What's the difference? None of us know what we're doing. We just know more than the public. They don't know what we know and what we don't." He continued, "It's like this—we're just actors in an Alpine Helen play. We're creating this pretend world, and hopefully the visitors will get lost in that world and want to come back over and over again."

David and Janet operated their little imported-candy store, adding a small handmade-fudge operation at a later date. In doing so, David became very knowledgeable about the candy business, which laid the groundwork for what would happen in the years to come. David was one of the first guys I met when coming to Helen, and we soon became friends. He was kind and supportive. He was also glad to have someone else his age with whom to play golf and tennis, and generally have fun. However, I also know he thought I was out of my mind to come to Helen for the golf-and-tennis business.

Over the years, we've laughed about me stopping by

his shop to give him one of my new orange T-shirts with BAVARIAN BROOK GOLF AND RACQUET CLUB printed on the front. I was young and excited without a thought of failing. Everyone else figured I was living on short time.

David, Charles, Pete, and I had daily afternoon golf outings. One of our favorite games was the old "create-a-hole" game. This is where the winner of the last hole makes up the next hole. It can start from anywhere and end at any one of the nine greens or the practice green. It was a great creative golf game. We were even known to include hitting at cars that were riding across our golf course instead of on the highway. Basically, whatever came to mind could be part of the play.

The game I remember best took place in early spring of '76 at Mr. MacGregor's Pizza House located across Highway 75 from the ninth fairway. It was to be our last hole of the day, and it was Pete's turn to choose the hole. After completing play on number eight, Pete said, "Let's drive across the highway to MacGregor's and get a beer before we finish up."

Off we went to MacGregor's side deck overlooking the highway for a nice, cold Pabst Blue Ribbon. After finishing, Pete got to his feet and asked us to help him move the table and chairs. Then he turned, walked down to his golf bag, and drew his three-wood for battle. "Okay, the game is, hit your tee shot off the deck, across the highway, down the bank, hopefully to the short grass midway down the number-nine fairway. From there, we drive over the island area to somewhere en route to the practice green in front of the clubhouse. It's a par four, boys."

We did it just like he said it, placing the ball upon the hard deck wood surface. Teeing off consisted of wood club hitting wood deck and a sound much like today's nail guns.

Oddly enough, all our tee shots were pretty good and ended up in the short grass. But the next shot was a tough one. We ended up with balls laying everywhere from high grass to the eighth tee and everything in between. David ended up way off to the right, almost on the seventh green, with the tennis court between him and the final goal, which was the practice green. Pete, Charles, and I all hit the green with our third shot. Then, it was David's shot. If we were lucky, he would dump it in the tennis court and the three of us would be left with a putt-off between us.

David stood over the ball, then took the club back and down through the ball. It popped high in the air, cleared the tennis-court fence on the practice-green side, hit the side of the green, and started running toward the hole. It rolled and rolled until we heard the final sickening *plop*. Ball in hole for birdie three.

We had a winner, but not the winner Pete, Charles, and I had in mind. Of course, David did the strut. "Just like I played it," he said. We just looked at each other thinking, *Why us, Lord, and why him?* David was always in the middle of everything, just like the rest of us. If it was fun, we did it.

After Pete's departure from this world, David played on. He was one of the few of us that really knew what Pete was doing and how he had gotten to where he had so quickly. He also knew that without Pete, we were in trouble. Years passed, and David's involvement increased with ups and downs. It was the typical growing crap: people not wanting others to get ahead of them, and jealousy, along with a big touch of greed and a lack of compassion. Those of us who had learned from Pete pushed forward, learning as we went, giving to the program rather than taking.

David was one of those chosen few. David and I would spend endless days and nights talking about our next steps forward. We watched locals try to grab property and investments to place themselves in superior financial positions. It was every man for himself, and we had to protect what we had poured our lives into. I had real estate, and David had a business.

It wasn't a comfortable feeling for us after Pete's death, but we overcame those hard times. I ended up in real estate and property management, and David built a candy empire. David became so successful, he was named to the board of directors of Retail Confectioners International and became its leader.

Next time you're in Helen, go see David at his Hansel & Gretel Candy Kitchen on Main Street. He'd love to see you. Just tell him Hue said to show you his candy. I can assure you, he will share it!

WINTER 1975-1976

The Story of the Village Inn

The first lodging in Helen was the Helendorf Inn located at the corner of Highway 75 and Edelweiss Strasse. It was built next to the river on the site of the main building of a long-departed lumberyard. It was also the first golf shop and overlooked the ninth green of the early Helen golf course, Georgia's only one-hole golf course.

However, in Pete's mind, he had to keep things progressing. Once one thing was begun and rolling, he moved on to the next. He loved to make things happen. Few people coming to Helen after 1980 have any idea of how the Village Inn Motel came to be or the part it played in the growth of Helen's Valley area. The Village Inn concept had all the markings of Pete's fast-moving style. His method of getting it underway would result in jail time today, but in 1975, it was just another game to be played.

In the fall of that year, Pete began work on the Valley's second lodging complex. He started the Village Inn Quadplexes, later to be known as the Village Inn Motel. The completed project would have five buildings of four units each. The first thing he did was pick a location. The natural choice was a project he had already begun at the island area with its water moat. He kept it filled by pumping water out of the nearby river until the moat was full or until the rains came. When the water level receded, he'd just fill her up again to about six feet deep at the deepest spot.

Lovell Engineering surveyed a spot of land for twenty-five building sites where Pete's quadplexes would be built. This would give the project a total of one hundred units and make it the largest rental property yet in Helen, even larger than the Helendorf Inn.

These quadplexes would be four units each, as the name states, and be of different Bavarian designs and colors. Each building would be a fee-simple title and be marketable to investors as a winning project with a positive cash flow. An investor could buy one building (or as many as he or she might desire) and be assured they would only have to make a down payment. If they wanted financing, it would be provided on the local level. In other words, it was a condo arrangement that Pete was careful not to call by that name. You don't want to cloud the thinking of locals and local officials.

After the site work was completed, Pete employed his friend J. Mundy to design the actual units. The five completed buildings you see today make up the total completed project; however, it is eighty units short of the originally designed amount.

Pete's next step was twofold. He needed a board of directors made up of owners to run and set policy for the venture. This is where some of us came in. Pete chose several of us to act as would-be owners and investors, giving him the clout and appearance of ready-and-willing investors. He picked his board from this group, and I was the chairman. Even my father got into the act, despite not having a clue what was going on. No money changed hands; it was just names on paper, but it was enough to convince a local lending institution he had an up-and-going venture. Of course, it also looked good to potential investors who might come in off the street for some of the action.

Now, one might think he was crazy to give stock to folks with no investment, but Pete always protected himself well. The fact was, we were all having so much fun in this pretend world that we never would have thought of taking advantage of Pete. We were so tied up with other aspects in his puzzle that doing Pete wrong wouldn't have been in our best interest. He held the trump card, anyway: he didn't even own the property! The Alpine Valley Investment Corporation did.

Money! With all this set up, Pete needed money, but where would he get it? Local banks, of course. They didn't trust Pete, nor did they believe in Helen, but they all liked him. He was the master at the art of the deal and could charm the sharpest of bankers at the drop of a hat. When Pete set out to get his financial way, not a bank was safe. With all the paperwork to back him up and one of his assistants at his side, he carefully planned out his full day of attack.

They set off toward Habersham County in his now-famous Chevy station wagon on the big day. I swear he used that car for everything from SUV (before there was such a thing) to golf cart. "A-banking we will go" would be his song of the day, and at day's end he would have what he went after: two construction loans.

Now, there's nothing unusual about getting a loan for a building, but borrowing money twice for the same building wasn't normal—and probably not legal, either. Each bank had lent him the money to build a quadplex, but what they didn't know was that it was the same building. This allowed him additional money to spend elsewhere.

When the bank folks came out to see how their building was going, he would show them around the building that they thought was the one they had financed. They weren't completely wrong, but they weren't completely right, either. Pete was careful that they didn't come at the same time. That's where his gambling spirit kicked in.

You're right: it is illegal. You say it couldn't happen, but I tell you, it did, and they never found out. Sooner rather than later, Pete came up with other funds from some other crazy method to build the second building, which gave both banks a building to back up their investments. Even then, it was hard for me to believe a bank could be so easily fooled.

In short order, the project was going and the stock certificates disappeared, along with all the links to our names. As I mentioned earlier, Alpine Valley Investment Corporation owned the property, not Pete. I'm sure Pete knew that the stockholders and officers of the corporation would also have been liable.

Pete died before this project could be completed, and the result is a five-building project that operates successfully today. If five buildings work, then twenty-five would have worked even better. Pete created, deceived, and produced a winner . . . just another of his games.

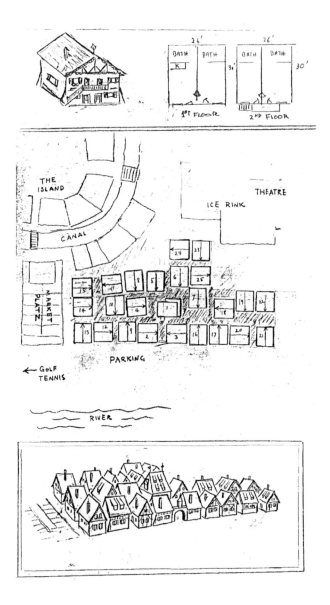

A sketch by artist John Kollock of the proposed Village Inn complex

Sketch courtesy of Nancy Kollock

The Devil Made Us Do It

Looking back over this period in Helen, I can't believe so many of us did some of the things we did. There seemed to be no limits, and fun was the game. Maybe it was because we could get away with it. In telling some of this, I hope the statute of limitations has run out on our transgressions. By today's standards, many of the main players in early Helen would have ended up in court over our fun and games, but we meant no harm.

One of our most interesting sports on a weekend evening was sign collecting. Sometimes there would be up to twenty locals competing in one of these late-night adventures. We would get together dressed in dark clothes, have a few drinks, and go for it. The bigger the sign was and the harder it was to get, the better you did. I don't know why. I guess it was just fun, and the good part was, we always returned our finds (to the people we liked).

Crazy!

We had another fun exploit with a different purpose altogether. If someone in town was bucking "our program," we would go into action. One example was a family who came to Helen and opened a pizza place. They were nice folks with great pizza, but they painted their roof yellow, which is a no-no in Helen. The Alpine theme required all roofs to be tiled red.

Now, I want to make this quite clear: This adventure was planned and ready for action . . . but it was *never* carried out.

We mixed up two five-gallon containers of old paint of a not-so-great color, got a ladder ready, and even made a practice run the night before the caper was to take place. Our plan was to put the ladder on the backside of the house, crawl to the ridge of the roof, and pour the paint down the visible side of the roof. It would have had to be fixed, and our hopes were that the city would require it to be fixed in red. We wanted them to get the message that the community players were not happy with their roof.

One thing I need to say is that Pete had no idea about this kind of stuff. It just wasn't his style. I guess the folks involved thought it would be helping him. To my knowledge, no one was ever caught or hurt. Nor did anyone else get hurt, and any expense we caused was very small. We looked at it as a matter of right and wrong for the group, but looking back, it wasn't too smart.

Gold Spikes Impress German Metal Working Horn Tooter

Helen Transit! Ever heard of it? I bet not, but it did exist in the winter of '76. In fact, there are still artifacts around which hint at the fact that Helen Transit was a going operation . . . or could have been a going operation in Helen. There was stock, a checkbook, a bank account, a streetcar sitting in Paris waiting to be delivered, and an event planned to drive a great gold spike to kick off the new transit authority. It was a publicity stunt in the making, right down Pete's alley.

Soon after I came to Helen in the summer of '75, I heard a story about the streetcar being built by an Atlanta artist and ski-club supporter in the Vinings area. After asking Pete about these rumors, he showed me a photograph of the first Helen Transit streetcar that was in Paris waiting to be shipped to our dear little village. He asked if I'd like to go to Atlanta with him now that I'd seen what thousands of others had seen, which had been written about in many newspaper ads. I accepted and asked why, to which I got a quick, sharp reply of "I'll show you when we get there."

We made our trip to Atlanta and found ourselves in a northern suburb with huge houses tucked among the acreage. We drove up a long, winding drive. There was an interesting ski run made of sawdust that I later found out the Atlanta Ski Club used to teach skiing. At the top of the hill and far off the road there was a large house with a workshop in the rear. Outside the shop, the streetcar stood in all its glory! It wasn't in Paris at all . . . but it made for a great story!

Later, as the weather turned bleak with winter, Pete set the date for the driving of the great gold spike. It was to announce the coming of the streetcar and the new, somewhat less-than-rapid Transit Authority. The ceremony would be in his office parking lot on a Saturday. Three veterans of the old Helen railroad days would be honored. They would drive the first spikes. Of course, everyone would be invited, especially the press.

Saturday came and so did the rain, but that wasn't a problem for Pete. The ceremony and the masses of invited guests headed inside his office. With the railroad ties, spikes, track, and sledgehammers painted gold, the ceremony was a success, despite the weather. It was quite a big deal, and the Helen Transit system was born, but the event did more than kick off a transit system that would never carry the first person anywhere. It also made a lasting impression on a couple living in South Florida.

This couple was from middle Germany, and like many Germans, they were smart, hard-working folks. They also had the ability to make a lot of money. He had already done quite well in the ornamental-iron business doing special work for southern Florida's wealthy folks.

Like so many of us during that period in Helen's evolution, they had a dream and the tools to make it come true. They had a German heritage, could play music, had money, as well as a desire to open an authentic German restaurant. They wanted out of South Florida, and Helen seemed to be their answer. The spike-driving ceremony made their decision just a little bit easier. Soon, they bought property and built a three-story restaurant with a bar and nightly entertainment, which they provided. They named it the Old Heidelberg Restaurant. Everything was authentic, from the German beer to the hand-prepared veal for the mouthwatering schnitzel.

This is just one more of the coming-to-Helen stories set in '75 and '76, another part of Pete's puzzle to make Helen the real thing with real folks. It started with a transit ceremony and ended with an authentic German restaurant in a Bavarian Alpine village in the middle of North Georgia with real German food and beer, owned by real German folks, who entertained with real German instruments playing real German music.

Who said we weren't the real thing?

Spare Tire and All, Including the Jackass

Sometime during the early spring of '76, a young couple arrived from somewhere to seek their fortune. Driving a big four-door Cadillac and sporting hair of special notice, they screamed *classy*. During the '75–'76 period, profit-seekers came from everywhere for every reason you could dream of. Of course, in Pete's mind, they were just another part of the puzzle to success, just a way to get from A to B.

One night about dark, Pete, David, and I were leaving the golf course from our daily game of choice when we spotted this overstuffed Cadillac with its out-of-place owners standing, looking helplessly at the three buildings in the island area. In fact, they were eyeing the one with the three flights of outside steps leading up to a small top-floor apartment. It wasn't hard to know what they were thinking with all that stuff and all those stairs. Pete pulled up next to these two poor, lost souls to assess the situation. The situation became very clear: they were moving in!

We sat watching for what would come next, and we weren't disappointed. The slick-haired man grabbed a box, as did Barbie Doll, and they made their way up the long climb. Home sweet home, at least for a while.

Pete said, "Looks like we got some new folks. Let's give them a hand."

We climbed out of the station wagon, grabbed their stuff, and followed them across the bridge and up the steps. When they saw the worker elves who'd appeared from the dark, they just looked in disbelief. I'm sure they must have thought of the Lone Ranger and Tonto. *Who are these masked men?*

We finished carrying our loads. David and I had boxes, which we set in the corner, and Pete had their spare tire, which he leaned carefully against the wall. We had completely emptied the trunk! They didn't even notice the tire as we departed without even introducing ourselves. We never did know what they thought of us; we just helped in a time of need and had a good laugh.

Barbie and Elvis lasted about two years in Helen. They opened a fake gold mine, complete with a real jackass. Her father came to town, opening a little shop that outlasted Barbie and husband. They all departed sometime after a local resident shot and killed the jackass. Some things don't need to happen. Damn rednecks!

Where those folks went, who knows? They did nothing wrong. Like so many others, I guess they thought there was gold in these here hills!

Helen's Atlantic

Once you're into ballooning, you have a whole wide world of contacts open up. It's like a completely new address book. At least, that's the way it was in the seventies if you were a balloonist. Pete was a balloonist. Somewhere in his book of contacts he made a connection with a strange, fast-talking guy who flew the Lark balloon. Remember the Lark cigarettes with their red-and-white pack?

Pete picked up on this dude and had an idea there was something to be gained for his Helen puzzle. Pete found out this Lark pilot had tried to fly the Atlantic in a hot-air balloon twice, but failed both times. The first time, he had to ditch in the ocean. The next time, his crew chief decided upon lift-off he was going, too, and jumped into the basket. This wasn't the plan, and caused a rapid end to attempt number two. Pete's idea was that Helen would sponsor this guy's next fly-the-Atlantic adventure. It would be great for publicity and carry us a notch further into the tourist world. He met with the balloonist, and the deal was made.

The balloon would be named "Helen's Atlantic" and would be red with white letters. To kick off the production (and it was just that), we would have a one-hundred-dollar-per-person dinner at the Hilton in Downtown Atlanta. Everybody who was anybody was invited. The gamut was set. With help, Pete set up the black-tie affair, and all bases were covered. He even chartered a bus to take Helen folks to the event, so we could make a giant entrance at the Hilton all together. I had told Pete that I couldn't afford the hundred bucks, and he quickly told me not to worry about it, just come on and let's do the town. We did.

I couldn't believe who was there. There were politicians, lawyers, state tourist leaders, newspaper folks, TV folks, and who knows who else. What a deal . . . or better said, what a sham. That's right, a sham. Pete had no plan of putting up money of this amount for anybody's Atlantic venture. If anyone else wanted to bankroll the adventure in the name of Helen, it was all right with him.

At the dinner, introductions were made, and then came the highlight of the evening: the unveiling of the model of "Helen's Atlantic." I can remember it just like it was yesterday. The pilot's young, little knockout, live-in girlfriend rolled the balloon model covered with a white sheet to the front of the head table. Everyone was staring. Their eyes were about to pop out looking toward the covered tray, but what they were looking at was the little honey with the skin-tight black dress with her boobs hanging out. She had long black hair and was almost more than the drunken crowd could take. She unveiled the model and it was nice, just like her. The pilot knew what he was doing when she became part of the act.

A few weeks later, "Helen's Atlantic" was history, but Pete had gotten more free publicity. Pete died before the Hilton was ever paid for the evening. This didn't affect me one way or the other, because I didn't pay anyhow. The ones that did pay just donated to the cause. No telling where Pete used the money. Maybe the pilot got some of it, after all.

The real truth of the matter was that this was the only time that I saw Pete get hold of someone that was as slick as he was. This pilot dude was slick, and for years later he would turn up with deals. I think that's the way he lived. To my knowledge, he never made another attempt on flying the Atlantic.

Helen's Untold Story

I've always said that the great thing about Helen is that there was never any big-money people involved in its success. Come to think of it, that's not quite true. The Atlanta Hilton bought us all dinner and a night out one winter night in '76, which resulted in thousands of dollars of free publicity. Here's to the big boys.

Flying across the Atlantic in a Balloon has never been done. 5 People have been killed in the last few years trying.

Thomas Gatch
- Malcolm Forbes

and many others have made the attempt to be the first person to fly across in a Balloon.

(Bob Sparks has made 2 attempts.)

FIRST.TIME..1973..The weather threw him into the ocean off of Newfoundland after 23 hours.
SECOND TIME..1975..Someone hung onto a line and dangled beneath his balloon on take off causing a helium leak.

Bob Sparks is making another attempt in June 1976 and has named his balloon for the Atlantic crossing..HELEN'S ATLANTIC

He has already explained to the national press that the reason he named his balloon HELEN'S ATLANTIC is because, "The same spirit and daring involved in rebuilding a town like Helen, Ga. is required in flying across the Atlantic."

Upon successful crossing of the Atlantic, Spark's balloon, HELEN'S ATLANTIC,will go into the Smithsonian Institute and be immortalized there. The same buildup and notoriety will be attached to Bob Sparks and HELEN'S ATLANTIC that we associate with Lindbergh and the SPIRIT OF ST. LOUIS. Such notoriety will vault Helen from a regional name to International Fame.

The State of Ga. was sufficiently impressed to participate with us in putting on a $ 100 a plate dinner in Atlanta at the new Atlanta Hilton with the proceeds going toward the expenses of the Atlantic crossing. The dinner is planned as a mammoth Press Kickoff for Bob Sparks and HELEN'S ATLANTIC with Bob explaining to the National Media why he selected Helen for the name of his balloon.

The dinner will be covered by the Wall Street Journal, New York Times, the Atlanta Newspapers, Gainesville Times, Helen Mountain Eagle, The Cleveland Courier, NewsWeek, Time Magazine, New Yorker Magazine, Southern Living, WSB radio, WGST radio, ABC-TV, CBS-TV, NBC-TV, Atlanta channel 17, and many others. The dinner will also line up the press for this years Balloon Race in Helen, Ga. (For which there are already 42 entries. Bob Sparks and Malcolm Forbes will both attend.)

DINNER INFORMATION

Date: Thursday Feb. 26,1976

Time: Reception.... 6 pm
        Dinner and
          Program.... 7 pm

Place: New Atlanta Hilton
        Grand BallRoom West

Price: $ 100 per plate (Second plate, wife or date..$ 25)

For further information call: Pete, Nancy or Janey   878-2269
                               Buz Lee   878-2629
                               Barbara Gay   878-2271

In addition to the tremendous promotional coverage, the dinner will be a gathering of Free Spirits of all sorts who will find Bob Sparks and the stories of his adventures and upcoming plans spine tingling.

NOTABLES

Doctor Tom

I had a battle with cancer in 1978. It showed me what it's like to be sick—to look okay, but not be okay. My illness also completely changed the way I thought about and lived my life. I started celebrating birthdays and thanking our Lord for every breath. It made me think every day of what I've offered and what I can still offer. This has been a hard thought for me, because even today, many years later, I'm not sure of the answer. Yet, I'm still trying, and feel I'm closer now than I was before.

With the help of some experimental drugs and the care of good doctors, nurses, family, and friends, I am a cancer survivor. I can't say enough about these folks, but there is one that rises above all—one who didn't have to do anything, but chose to help someone he really didn't know that well.

Doctor Tom Tidmore and his wife, Marion, were early investors and supporters of Alpine Helen. They were longtime friends of John Kollock, a local artist and one of the founders of Alpine Helen. Their second home was near the Kollock's place. Being major investors in the Helendorf Inn and other real estate projects, Tom and Marion kept up with John's exciting creation. Throughout the early days of Alpine Helen, they were involved in different projects, some of which did well and others which didn't. Yet, these pioneers believed in the concept and were on board 100 percent. Tom was also the chief anesthetist at Egleston Children's Hospital at Emory. He was well known in medical circles and respected for his superior work in the medical field.

After I found out about the tumor in my right testicle,

a friend dropped me off at Crawford W. Long Memorial Hospital in Downtown Atlanta. All by myself and scared to death, I entered the hospital and checked myself in. Things like that help the growing-up process.

I got my room and waited for a visit from my doctor. I was scheduled for surgery to remove the testicle, which my doctor had told me had a 90 percent chance of being malignant. My phone rang. Tom was on the other end telling me not to worry; he had made arrangements for one of his best students to be my anesthetist, and I would be well taken care of. And I was!

The next morning they drugged me, and away I went to the operating room, still scared to death and still by myself. As we entered the operating area, a woman concealed by a surgical mask and head covering met me to say, "Hue, it's okay. Doctor Tom said for me to take good care of you."

You could have knocked me over with a feather. Good ol' Doctor Tom had gotten me a lady anesthetist to take care of me during an operation on my private parts. She was a masked lady, to boot, and as they once said about one of my favorite childhood TV programs, "Who was that masked man? Why, it was the Lone Ranger!"

In my case, it was "Who is this masked lady?" I think it was Dr. Tom's favorite student.

Now, picture what was going through my mind for my first-ever surgery. First, it was for the removal of something most guys wouldn't talk about, which is a bunch of crap. Next, this operation was in front of a lady student anesthetist, and its subject was below the belt, so to speak. It was being performed by a Greek doctor, and to top it all off, there's a gay, black guy making jokes as he prepped me. I was totally out of control and didn't have any idea how I would come out of this. One thing's for sure: it would be with one less ball and most likely with cancer.

Think about that for a minute.

I hurt when I woke up in the recovery room, and then they took me to my room. By now I had a guest, and the being alone was over. I also found out that my special anesthetist had done just what she had set out to do in taking the best care of me. She had given me just the right amount of stuff to come out of it with no side effects. One hour after returning to my room, I ate a full lunch with no sickness. In fact, I ate at noon and got out of bed and walked by myself one hour later.

How about that, sports fans?

The next morning, with a room full of visitors, this gorgeous creature, about five eight with long, blonde, flowing hair and a killer body, entered my room saying, "Hue, how are you this morning?" After I managed a positive answer, she replied, "I told you that I'd take care of you."

It was only the beginning of being taken care of by these amazing people. While waiting for a wicked lymph-system test, which was more like torture, the phone rang again, and once again Doctor Tom came to the rescue. He had used his professional influence to line me up with the head of urology at Emory Medical Center, which resulted in a major exploratory operation to limit the possibility of the cancer spreading through the lymph system. The whole thing was horrible, but resulted in a clean lymph system. The only possibility of a future spread was through the blood system, which happened three months later. After this came chemo, infection, and all that goes with it, but I'm here today and proud of it.

Dr. Tom Tidmore

Photo courtesy of Barbara Gay

SPRING 1976

We Believe in Our Carousel

Looking back over the years, it's funny to remember the lack of support and confidence lending institutions and banks had in the change and development of Georgia's Alpine village. They thought it would fall flat and fail. With this kind of support, Pete had more challenges than he needed. Of course, he could dream up about every way possible to suck money from sources. He was a master at creating success out of the impossible.

One of the impossible ventures was the Helendorf Inn. It was born with the strength of doctors, lawyers, and chiefs from all over. From its beginning until the present, this inn has been a giant in the Helen lodging industry.

Throughout the history of Helen, there have never been any two people who believed in and supported Pete's adventures more than Tom and Marion Tidmore. These wonderful folks from Atlanta were among the first to be involved, and remained so until the nineties, when Tom died.

In Tom's last years, the Sautee Valley and the community center became their focus. Marion continued supporting the local area in a new century. I put folks into two categories: the givers and the takers. The Tidmores top the list of the givers. They were early investors in the Helendorf Inn, as well as many other endeavors around the area. Whatever Pete needed, they were there to help. Of all their widespread support for Pete's development, it was their smallest venture that is the most notable in my memory: the carousel.

Sometimes our dreams and desires get in the way of our better judgment, and that's when we step out beyond the limits of reality. This carousel idea was just such a desire and not really one of Pete's major causes . . . although he always said the more that was happening, the better.

Tom and Marion owned a moat lot, and they contracted with a contractor from Lake Burton to build this little carousel their longtime friend John Kollock had designed for them. It had numerous colors and was round in design with a flag on top. It was a circular building on a concrete slab that consisted of about eight triangular stalls. It was designed for vendors to sell their arts and crafts out of the stalls. They saw this as a homemade kind of arts-and-crafts fair to promote the struggling island area of town.

Unfortunately, there was a lack of foot traffic in the area around the carousel. The Tidmores pressed on in hopes of success, but in the end, it never came for that particular project. The carousel later became a unique storage building.

The carousel is long gone with no sign of its existence, just a memory of one effort among many. After this failing effort, with little to no regret about the carousel, they regrouped and reinvested in many other Helen projects, including a business that lasted for years in the island area, the Kite Site.

It's common knowledge that many doctors aren't good business people, but the good Doctor Tom was an exception. It's also generally known that most successful men have a strong woman behind them. Those of us that know Marion will always give her that credit, and more.

The Great Easter-Olive Hunt

With the rebirth of plants, flowers, and the seasons changing, Easter is a special time of year. My favorite time of the year is spring, a season of renewal. Easter is also the time of year when believers take stock of our beliefs. We hang on to the promises that we base our lives upon. It's a special time.

This time of year, most folks get anxious to get out and about, to do things and go places. Kids head to the beach for fun, wild times, and last but not least, the sun. We older folks think about what the sun can do to us, whether it's skin cancer, sunburn, or just plain old wrinkles. However, just like the kids, we like to have a little fun, so in the spring, getting together comes natural. We do this by cooking out and partying in the good ol' outdoors. Golfers and tennis players take to the links and courts while the little kiddos can't wait until the great egg is left by the Easter Bunny. Easter-egg hunts are a way of life, but back on Easter Sunday of 1976, some of us had an Easter-egg hunt of a different kind in mind.

Since most of us had at least attended sunrise services, we gathered at Pete's office to see how we might spend the rest of this beautiful day. There were about twelve of us sitting around, thinking about the crazy Saturday we had just spent. It was a day when our friend from Atlanta had entertained us with his horse of a different type: his motorcycle. We had all been gathered at Pete's the previous day to enjoy some sunshine that the long, freezing winter had robbed us of when Larry Woods pulled in on his motorcycle after driving up from Atlanta. Of course, everyone wanted a ride, which wasn't the best thing for Larry, since he didn't have an extra helmet.

"Not a problem," said Pete, and off he went to some unknown place. After a few minutes, he returned and said, "Let's take a ride."

How, you might ask? Pete had rented a wagon for the day, so we could hitch Larry's motorcycle to the front of the wagon and all take a ride around town.

One tourist commented, "Only in Helen."

So, the next day we were there at the same spot. What were we going to do to entertain ourselves and the tourists today? Once again, Pete came through. "Let's have an Easter-olive hunt! Larry, you're the Great Easter-Olive Priest."

We wrapped two dozen large, pitted olives in Handy Wrap. One of Pete's assistants hid them out in front of the office for all the world to see. Pete got all the Easter-olive hunters together with their Easter baskets and gave them the rules of the day. With several pitchers of martinis made and ready to drink, each hunter was given a full glass. A hunter had to crawl on hands and knees with the full glass in one hand while hunting for olives with the other. Upon finding an olive, you had to drop it into the full glass and chug the contents, including your prized olive, until your glass was empty. Then, you had your glass refilled and did it all over again. The hunter finding the most olives was declared the winner of the Great Easter-Olive Hunt and awarded another martini.

I couldn't tell you who won, because at the end of the hunt, it made little difference. This event was never repeated, most likely because there never was anyone like Pete to dream it up. Anyhow, it would have never been as good the second time around.

Developers, Not Promoters!

It was early April, and golf was in the air. Pete was a golfer with his own style. He was also a gambler who could and would bet anything on anything. His golf game was a talent he could depend on to back his crazy bets. His golf clubs were a thing of wonder; they looked like something he'd found or maybe purchased at Goodwill. They were a mixed mess of all types and brands, with some in bad need of repair. They were joined by an assortment of various types of golf balls in a canvas bag with broken zippers. An unknowing opponent would be quick to accept or make a gaming bet with a so-called golfer carrying equipment of this nature. It was a genuine set of tools for a true gambler. Looking at Pete's junk clubs, he appeared to be an easy take. There was a surprise yet to come.

The way Pete played golf was the way he played most games—and lived his life, to boot. He would describe most everything as a game. If he was going banking, it was a game, as was dealing with would-be investors. He liked to label himself as *just a* country boy. His friend/business partner, Lanier Chambers, was *just a* farmer. Being in the *just a . . .* category made them seem easy targets. Once again, a surprise was yet to come.

Giving him an edge to accomplish the impossible, he could use deception and elusion to even things up. Pete could get things done like no other person I've ever met. Most labeled him as a promoter, but he was far more than that. In fact, he hated being known as a promoter. He wanted to be a developer.

In early spring of 1976, Pete had so much going on, keeping up with him was a day-and-night job. And that's just about what he did: worked day and night. I can remember driving back from Atlanta in the early hours of the morning, only to see Pete sitting on the hood of his car with a legal pad, making notes of what's next. His mind was like a computer, endlessly spitting out ideas and solutions to problems.

One special trait he had was the ability to find a good opportunity for most everyone. He would meet a person, and before the day was over (if it even took that long), he had found a place for the person to fit into his master plan. He only needed what they could offer. They didn't have to be the perfect person; they just needed to have a quality that fit his needs. He treated everyone the same way. He didn't hurt them; he just used them for his best benefit. Most didn't even have a clue.

Spring was moving forward rapidly with the construction of the Village Inn quadplexes, the sale and construction of the island shops, the opening of the golf-and-tennis center as well as the Christmas shop, and the cutting and paving of a secondary road and a parking lot. There were many more items, all of which Pete called "eye wash." Knowing how badly he needed a break and that golf was his weakness, I invited him to go with me to Hilton Head. We'd stay at my father's condo, see the Heritage Classic golf tournament, and play a little golf. He needed some time away, and he accepted my invitation.

We lit out in my Coupe de Ville to join Dad and a doctor friend of his. It was the last golf tournament being played before the Masters in Augusta. All the big names were sharpening their games for one of the grand-slam events. Really, we could have cared less, because we were looking forward to playing a little golf ourselves.

After we arrived and settled in, I introduced Pete to Doctor Burn, who at that time was the head of therapy at the VA hospital in Decatur. Everyone hit it off, and our trip was up and going. Pete started the conversation about Helen in a way that invited questioning. It was his usual, low-key approach.

The second evening, Pete mentioned that he'd like to watch the evening news on NBC. No one objected, and at six o'clock it came on. Lo and behold, it included a special segment about a small Northeast Georgia ghost town coming back to life. It went something like this:

> "Tonight, we have an amazing human interest story about a small Northeast Georgia mountain town that has transformed itself into an Alpine village in five short years. But what's more amazing is that it was done without any government funding or even any major investors. Local money and local people combined to turn the former ghost town into one of Georgia's top-five tourist areas."

You should have seen the three of us. We looked at each other, then at Pete. I said, "Pete, that's got to be us!"

With a smile, Pete replied, "Yeah, I thought tonight was the night for it to air. And the best part is, it's nationwide primetime coverage. Didn't cost us a penny. It's the kind of advertising we couldn't dream of buying."

We watched until forty-five minutes had expired, with every break leading up to the final feature story. Then came fifteen full minutes of a story done in a way that a viewer in Helen wouldn't have believed possible. Presented by the nation's best-known reporters, you couldn't help but wonder how a little North Georgia mountain town could be so important. Looking back over the millions and millions of people who have visited, moved to, written about, and filmed the pretend world of Helen, it's easy to see ... *now*.

The good Doctor Burn felt he was staying in the same condo with a celebrity rather than my blue-jean-clad, Old-Navy-golf-shirt-dressed friend. As for Pete, it was just another day's surprise adventure, and a game played and won.

Our trip was to watch the Heritage Classic, but first we went to tee up at the Sea Marsh course at Sea Pines Resort and play a round. It was the premiere Hilton Head resort of the seventies.

Before placing the ball on its tee at the number-one hole, Pete asked, "What's the game? What do you want to play for?"

I was a pretty good golfer at the time, but I wasn't a gambling golfer. I also knew he was, and when standing over a big money putt, I wasn't in his class. I answered, "Pete, you and I made a deal for me to come to Helen. You asked me to do certain things for you, and in turn you would do certain things for me, and we're doing them. I can afford to keep up my end of the bargain. But if I let you take me on the golf course, it might be a different story."

He was quick to laugh, and before another word could come out of my mouth, he said, "How about a dollar per hole, no carryovers?"

And that was the game we played from that day on. In fact, that's the game I still play with my friend and fellow Helen supporter David Jones, "the candy man."

Over the next three days, we played three rounds of golf, fifty-four holes in all, and ended up all even between us. In fact, I believe that's the way it went up until his death. I've always known if the bets had been, let's say, ten dollars per hole, it would have been a different story. Remember, he liked games and lived to win.

During the trip, Pete called back to Helen several times to check on things. With his assistants in the office, he had good help, but he was still the final word. After one such call, he was laughing. Seems the new family moving to Helen from up north to open a first-class Christmas shop had arrived. A couple of Polish decent from the north with two wild little boys and big dogs had showed up carrying all their belongings in an Allied Van Lines moving truck. The house Pete had found for them, known locally as the Hurt House, was on the other side of the river. To get across, you had to use a small steel bridge, for which this particular truck was both too large and too heavy.

Needless to say, Pete's assistants had their hands full. If Pete had been there, it would have been another game, which he would have enjoyed and easily won. But he wasn't anywhere near, and the assistants would have to handle it, which they did.

Pete gave them some words of wisdom to take care of it. The large truck was unloaded at the bridge, then large forces of the locals turned out in Jeeps and pickup trucks. Each was decked out with gun racks and other redneck stuff, and they came to help move smaller loads across the old steel bridge. The snooty Christmas-shop family got a firsthand welcome from the good old boys. They, in turn, got a laugh and all the PBR they could drink (and boy, could they drink).

Pete and I both hated to miss it. We were sure it became the social event of the year. His assistants did a good job, and I'm sure they accepted the resulting celebration as reward for "super service under extreme fire."

The other thing we were supposed to do during our visit to Hilton Head was watch the professional golf tournament, and we did. It was great, but once again, the unexpected happened. As Dad, Dr. Burn, Pete, and I walked up to the eighteenth green to see who was finishing their round, one of the golfers spoke to Pete. It was Tommy Aaron from Gainesville, a past Masters champion. Pete knew the whole family. I was sure he'd played one of his high-stakes games of golf with them in the past. Tommy was finishing his round and heading for the clubhouse.

When we got to the clubhouse, Ron Kirby's wife was standing with Tommy. Ron was the golf-course architect who worked with Gary Player designing golf courses. Their company had designed the nine-hole course in Helen, which today no one knows was ever there, but it was, and it seems that Ron Kirby never got his full pay. I'm not sure if he ever got much of anything. Pete informed me he'd best keep his eye out so as not to run into Ron Kirby. We kept our eyes open and didn't run into Ron.

Thinking our trip had ended way too soon, we headed up the road back to North Georgia. Pete shared with me his latest decision about two hours into the return trip. He had already called Paul Jr. to give him the go ahead to pave the road from the Helendorf Inn at Highway 75 to follow the river all the way past the island area to dead end at my front door. He was going to make a large paved parking lot in the area between the island shops and the river, running from the new Village Inn quadplexes to my Bavarian Brook Golf and Racquet Club. When it came down to the day of paving, he even did my walks and cart paths.

Of course, my first thought was, *How you going to pay for it?* He hadn't figured that part out yet, but he did, as usual. He said the paving would be black, but thin. He just needed it black for what he described as "eye wash." It wasn't just a means of getting from point A to point B, because he would use this new pavement to get something else going. Nothing like progress. Always progress.

The next week, it was done. It was nice and black, nice and thin, and wasn't paid for, but he did it somehow.

On that return trip, Pete confided in me about many things, but the thing I remember best was more of a desire or wish than anything else. It had to do with the way he was thought of and received. He said, "You know, all the things I do and the people I come in contact with, they all know me as a promoter, but what I really want to be is a developer. Somehow, I'm always a promoter."

This want-to-be developer was a promoter, and a damn good one. Actually, he was much more. He was a dreamer who would use every possible angle to turn dream into reality. He got things done when others couldn't even imagine them. He could be described so many ways, but perhaps all the descriptions should be mulled together to form a more suitable and worthy description of this very special man.

The Great Bike Race

It was early spring of '76, and all the young, sports-minded free spirits of Helen were making their way out of the winter blues. My first winter in Helen living over the golf-and-tennis shop had been a cold one, due to the fact that I only had an open fireplace and an electric heater in my small upstairs apartment. Much of my winter had been spent fixing new water pipes that had fallen victim to below-freezing weather. But now, spring was springing, and it was time for action.

Tennis, golf, and canoeing were all on the docket. Soon, the Helen-to-Atlanta canoe race would be here, but for many of us, it wasn't nearly soon enough. What could we do before the canoe race to create interest and press?

This one was my idea and mine alone. I get all the credit for the idea, but Pete provided much of the wisdom that led to success. He just seemed to always be there with the right answers. I went to Pete with this wonderful idea of having a street-bike race on a Saturday afternoon. Beginning in the center of town, the racers would make the loop to Robertstown, turn right at Unicoi State Park, make a right on to Skylake Road, take yet another right on Highway 255 en route to the Old Sautee Store. Once there, one more right on Highway 17 would take them down to the Nacoochee Indian Mound, where the final right would send them screaming to the same point where they had begun: the crosswalk in the center of town at Brown's Alpine Service Station. It was a complete circle of about nineteen miles, and I thought it would take about two hours to complete.

As I was running this by Pete, I had questions about how to pull it off and get the most out of it. Pete, being a master of getting results from anything, began to map out a plan. Pete said the first thing to do was go to the Chamber of Commerce and tell them what I wanted to do and ask them to be cosponsors of the event. He said to give the chamber all the credit they would take, and ask for their typical publicity. Pete said he would get one of his assistants to help with a press release to provide to the chamber, so they could pass it on to all the papers. After that, their work would be done, and they would feel like a true part of the plan.

Now, I was all set to go!

We had a route for the race, and we had the publicity covered so that pretty soon the entire town would know about the upcoming event. Next, we needed television-and-newspaper coverage. This part was a little outside my area of expertise, but having worked with Pete for about nine months, I knew there was a rabbit in the hat somewhere.

Over a late-afternoon beer, Pete and I went over the television possibilities. Phil Flynn had a weekly human-interest program by the name of *The Georgia Camera*. He and his cameraman had become special friends of Helen due to our efforts at making them comfortable when they visited. Our hospitality had provided good old TV coverage for free to us on a regular basis.

Phil's introduction to Helen came by way of another Pete player of the era, Larry Woods. Larry was an Atlanta television personality and the coeditor of the first modern-day newspaper in the Helen/White County area, the *Mountain Eagle*. We met with Larry and discussed our needs, and he took over from there. Seems that Phil's cameraman, Leroy, was in need of a little weekend vacation.

His wife had just had a baby, and a getaway was in order. If we could give Leroy and his wife a free weekend in Helen, there was no telling what we could get in the way of publicity. We did, and Leroy paid us back in spades!

Now that we had gotten Leroy to agree to film the race, we needed to get as much out of his work as possible. I contacted a friend in Atlanta who had designed my Bavarian Brook complex and who happened to have a great-looking Triumph TR6 sportscar. He agreed to bring his car up to act as the so-called pace car—cameraman in tow—to guide the bikers through town and on their way. He gave Leroy the best filming location possible.

We now had a way to film the race, but how did we get it on TV? Larry and Pete took care of this with a couple calls to Atlanta TV stations. In those days, all three main stations were fighting over the best coverage of odd happenings in Georgia, and Helen always came through with strange, off-the-wall events that were good for local ratings. Of course, Larry being employed by one of the stations didn't hurt at all, so when the race happened, they were waiting on the film. Once they got it, we made primetime at 6 p.m. and 11 p.m. on a Saturday night.

What about the newspaper? No problem! We had friends in all the right places. Phil Garner, a good friend of Larry's and his coeditor at the *Mountain Eagle*, wrote for the Atlanta paper, and he made some calls. We only had a few little things left to cover. You know, the rules and things like that. But there was at least one more surprise in store for us. When we finalized the list of competitors, we ended up with two professional, world-class riders who just happened to read the press release in Athens.

The race itself was a thing of beauty. Of the fifteen entries, ten finished, and all within sixty-seven minutes.

Remember, I thought the race would take more like two hours. What did I know? It was only an idea. A little of Pete had rubbed off on me.

Picture this: Pete and I were standing in the center of town at the start/finish line. Pete had the checkered flag and I had the stopwatch. After a little more than forty-two minutes, two riders topped the last hill and came speeding for the finish, side by side and pedal to pedal. Seconds later, Pete waved them across the finish with Dieball edging out Dailey by half the length of his front tire. These two world-class riders had put on an unforgettable show, which they had enjoyed as much or more than we did. And we had it all on film.

While eating their after-race bananas, Dieball and Dailey turned to me and asked if we could make the race two laps next year.

There never was a next year for the race.

Some other notable race results were Jeff Threlkeld and Ricky Abernathy, both local high school boys who started and finished the race. Jeff finished fourth in just fifty-two minutes. He was only two minutes behind Thompson, who finished in fifty minutes. Ricky, a classmate of Jeff's, finished ninth after crashing at the Highway 255 intersection, where Larry Woods, the tenth-place finisher, stopped to help. Larry said that he thought the kid was hurt, and the next thing he knew, Ricky was pedaling toward Helen. Ricky finished in sixty-six minutes, one minute before Larry. Our local journalist Phil finished seventh in fifty-seven minutes.

When we interviewed Larry and Phil afterward, they could hardly walk, and neither of them made any suggestions about adding a lap in the future. Their thoughts were more of the hot-tub-and-stiff-drink variety. One very important note is one of the top finishers was a girl who beat a lot of guys, and she was prettier, too!

One other bit of interest was our race-safety team. We had the civil defense lead the race with their old CD truck. It was the 1976 mountain model of today's EMT units. We thought that by having it in front of the racers, it could clear traffic. The problem was that on one big hill, the racers passed and outran the truck, leaving it far behind. It finished last and won no prize.

It was a great event and a wonderful day in Helen. We huddled in front of our TV sets to see the free publicity we got from our fun. Two days of weekend TV and newspaper coverage that we'd earned with just an idea—it was the Helen way.

I'd like to honor the memory of two people who played a vital role in this particular episode in Helen. Phil Flynn of *The Georgia Camera* passed on some years ago and is truly missed. Leroy, his cameraman, went on to a fine career in local TV with his own show, *The Leroy Powell Show*. He did this for years, entertaining folks by being himself. He, too, passed on in the nineties. I used to see Leroy from time to time when I went to Atlanta to promote Helen on the *Good Day Atlanta* show. We always laughed about the day we had on that April Saturday, and about how simple it once was, because we were just having fun.

ANNUAL
HELEN MARATHON
BIKE RACE

Saturday April 24
Starting Time 2:00 pm

RACE RUN UNDER USCA RULES

2 Classes (Geared & Non-Geared)
19 Mile Track Thru Mountains

ENTRANCE FEE $5.00 Per Entree

PRIZES
TROPHIES & GIFT CERTIFICATE

FINAL REGISTRATION 1 HOUR PRYOR TO RACE
OR MAIL CHECK WITH NAME & CLASS YOU WISH TO ENTER TO

BIKE RACE
BOX 333
HELEN, GEORGIA 30545

bavarian brook
GOLF & RACQUET CLUB

Helen to Atlanta, the Old-Fashioned Way

Spring saw events, events, and more events. Events by land, by air . . . and then there was water, good old Chattahoochee River water. How about a race from Downtown Helen to the I-285 bridge in northern Atlanta?

May of 1976 brought the third annual boat race to Atlanta. Like the previously held bike race and the balloon race still to come, this open-boat canoe race was another Helen happening that proved just odd enough to draw buckets of publicity. After all, that's what we did in Helen at every opportunity: generate free publicity.

The race would feature boats and paddlers of all sorts, including a seventeen-foot aluminum beauty carrying me and Charles, my Miami canoeing buddy. Our canoe was a big, heavy, monster of a whitewater craft. We were one of seventeen boats entered in the event. After beginning dead last, my navigational abilities led us to Atlanta in twenty-two hours and twenty minutes, a time good enough for seventh place. It was a satisfying feeling to complete the journey, and a hell of a good time, too.

Dave Gale, our race organizer and a transplant from Atlanta's engineering world, had moved to Helen a couple years earlier to open an outfitters shop. He and Anne had found a whole new life just eighty-five miles up the road, and as good folks who knew a lot of Atlanta people, they fit perfectly into Pete's plan. Dave's paddling partner just happened to be our good friend Phil Garner, who worked at the Atlanta paper and owned a local one, the *Mountain Eagle*. With Phil literally on board, publicity for the race grew with each stroke of the paddle. Seems Dave had learned a little something from Pete, as well.

Charles and I, being the golf-and-tennis nuts, allowed ourselves to be drawn into a friendly wager with Phil and Dave on who would get to Atlanta first. We jumped at the chance as their egos put one hundred bucks on the line. Neither Charles nor I had a spare hundred to our name, but we acted like the bet needed to be more. We were all bluff!

Race day came, and we all placed our boats by the river next to Pete's office before walking to the starting line at the top of town. The gun sounded, and we all dashed through Downtown to board our crafts and sprint through the Helendorf rapids in our race to the Workman's Bread House finish line. This first leg determined our starting positions down river near the Nacoochee Indian Mound.

Charles and I had already decided to take our own good time and begin the race in last place. We figured starting in dead last would make us look as though we didn't have a chance, which most of our friends believed anyway. The real reason for our slow start had to do with our wardrobe. I had us both dressed in bright-orange Bavarian Brook Golf and Racquet Club T-shirts and matching baseball hats. I wanted all the tourists to get a really good chance to read the advertisement while we saved our energy. After all, there was over one hundred miles of paddling to be done.

Dry and rested, we began in last place while Dave and Phil were nowhere to be seen. They were somewhere ahead of us, probably pretty sure of being one hundred dollars richer. You see, we had worked hard preparing for our journey, and by the time we passed Smith Island, we had moved up to eleventh place and were still dry. We had taken routes no one would have dreamed of, but they were within the rules. In fact, we had passed Phil and Dave before getting to the Clarkesville–Cleveland Bridge.

In the next stretch, Phil and Dave overtook us before we reached Duncan Bridge. They looked like they had been through the ringer. Giving it everything they had paddling their brand-new, low-draft, yellow racing canoe, they worked their way ahead. We just continued our smooth, effortless J-strokes down the river, heading on our merry way to Gainesville.

Soon, and to our delight, we rounded a bend where the yellow racing craft was beached. Dave was throwing up and Phil was suffering from leg cramps. We waved and gave them a typical "How you boys doing?" comment. We even went so far as to open our beer supply and offer them one. They, in turn, gave us some kind of hand motion that didn't seem like a wave. We just J-stroked our way down the river toward Atlanta.

They caught us again in the Gainesville stretch, where the '96 Olympic paddling events would be held years later, and finished the leg about five minutes before us. As we pulled into shore, they had nothing to say. We all ate fish together that evening in Gainesville, and Dave wasn't a happy camper. He knew then we were for real, and his hundred dollars didn't look such a sure bet anymore. The golf-and-tennis boys had become paddlers also. We were happy!

We went back to Helen for the evening and got some rest. We were back at the put-in spot at 8:00 a.m. for our Lake Lanier run to the dam. I had it all planned out on my waterproof map. I had taken a ruler and drawn straight lines from point to point, giving us the shortest possible route. It looked real strange, however. Common sense and my engineering ability told me that the shortest distance between two points is a straight line. All we needed was a windless day and we had it. We departed at 8 a.m. and began working our way across the lake.

The previous year, Pete had flown his yellow bird plane over the boat race and dropped small parachutes loaded with beer into the racing boats. This year we waited, but he was a no-show, so we made two quick stops at different marinas on our way to the dam.

From time to time we would see a canoe way off-course to the left. It was the last glimpse we would see of those confused racers, because we were Atlanta bound. At 3:00 p.m., seven hours from our put-in at Clark's Bridge, we reached Buford Dam. We ran up the dam to the top, crossed the road, and slid the boat down the grass backside of the dam. We jumped in the canoe, caught the dam release, and flew toward Atlanta.

We took out at Holcomb Bridge Road just three hours after getting off the lake. We pulled our boat out, stashed it in the bushes, and walked up to a minute market, where I called a friend of mine who lived in Roswell. This friend was the same one that had done all my drawings for my buildings, and he'd just returned from doing work in the Middle East. While there, he'd obtained a water pipe for smoking hash.

I knew he sounded strange on the phone, but he assured me he would be able to pick us up for the night. He showed up three hours later, and he was real smoked up. He was only about ten miles from us when I called him, but he drove all the way to Buford Dam—among other places—to find us. At 9:00 p.m. he fulfilled his mission and took us to his condo. The next morning, he had us back at our boat at put-in time, and we headed to Morgan Falls Dam.

There, we made the difficult portage and headed down the

last stretch for the Mooring take-out on the other side of I-285. It had been twenty-two hours and twenty minutes. We finished seventh out of all boats and first for boats of our class. Dave and Phil finished sixth, about thirty minutes before us.

As far as we were concerned, we had proved our point, and the feeling was unbelievable. I was on such a high that I could have paddled upstream all the way back to Helen. Of course, that would have gotten old quickly. It was the first and last time Charles or I would do this either together or apart. We had no idea what was in store for the remainder of May. It would be a lot of excitement, but not the good kind.

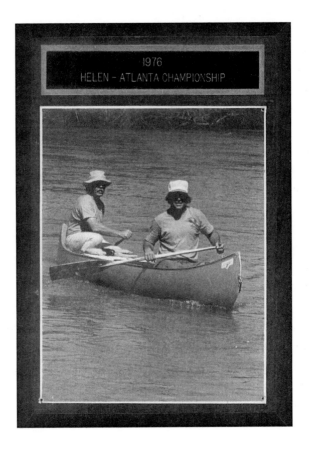

1976
HELEN – ATLANTA CHAMPIONSHIP

A YEAR END

Our Balloon Burst

Ballooning and Helen were one and the same. In fact, one of the first hot-air balloons in the state of Georgia was the original Helen balloon, which was a white cross set upon a red background on all sides, commonly known as the Swiss cross. It was made by Adams Ballooning out of Atlanta and classified as an experimental project. The top was like a duffle bag with a drawstring, and get this—it was held together with a short metal pin that was normally tied by a piece of grass. This drawstring then trailed all the way down the balloon, where it was fastened to the side of the basket for easy access for the pilot. It was the safety device that kept the top from coming open if the grass tie broke.

It wasn't nearly as primitive as it sounds. In ballooning, during dangerous and high-wind conditions, there are times you need to "pop the top." When this happens to allow hot air to escape, the "safety line" is released while the pilot feeds it out to acquire the desired size of opening in the top. Sometimes a balloonist will find that a short, quick fall is much better than what he's getting ready to hit. Take it from me. I've been there, done that!

A balloon basket can normally carry the pilot and one or two more folks. There are also up to four propane tanks (hopefully full of fuel), as well as other required instruments for safe flight. And I almost forgot the burners, which are located directly over the center of the basket and in the middle of the bottom opening to the giant balloon. Once these propane burners are fired, the lift comes from heating the air inside the balloon, resulting in an aircraft that's lighter than air.

That's a short, simple explanation of ballooning, and this little bit of technical knowledge will help you as you continue the story.

Pete had a hot-air balloon and used it as a wonderful promotion tool to attract attention to his pet project, Helen, Georgia's Alpine village. It didn't hurt that he promoted himself in the process. The balloon was simply a movable billboard that could and did turn up anywhere and everywhere. It was also fun and exciting, which was of utmost importance.

In 1974, Pete had created a balloon race to gain some attention. It was named the Helen to the Atlantic Balloon Race. This no-holds-barred race was what he called the race from the center of the earth (Helen) to the edge of the earth (the Atlantic Ocean).

Generally, in Helen, the prevailing winds would blow toward the Atlantic somewhere between the Outer Banks and Jacksonville. Who knew? And honestly, what difference did it make? Pete wasn't interested in the winner. He was more interested that the event drew press from newspapers to television stations, and once the balloons were inflated, there was media coverage. The greatest part was, it was free, and led with the name Helen, Georgia's Alpine village. Another viewpoint is it was like an adult/kids' adventure game, where any and everybody could be involved. The more you landed and took off, the more folks got involved, and they never forgot.

In Helen, being the kind of pretend world it was, Pete wasn't the only one who had a balloon. His partner in crime, Lanier, had an even bigger and more colorful balloon made by a different maker. It was known as the

Kaleidoscope balloon. I never knew the arrangement between Pete and Lanier, but both would fly whichever balloon they could get to first. I'm sure two balloons were better than one.

In the seventies, ballooning in our area was an adventure consisting of fun, partying, and beer. No pilot had a license or logbook to keep records of flights. Rules only got in the way of our playtime. Everything was by the seat of your pants, and the last thing you wanted was a record of the flight. The Helen area was an FFA nightmare, and rightfully so.

In 1974, the first balloon race was held with four balloons. While my dad and I were getting lumber at Mt. Yonah Lumber Company for our project at Lake Burton, I remember seeing one balloon after another come over Mount Yonah. It was an unbelievable sight, to see those balloons floating over the mountains.

The Forbes balloon, piloted by the world-renowned pilot and millionaire Malcomb Forbes, took the lead. Next came the Budweiser balloon with Senator Tom Rutherford from New Mexico. Behind them came Pete and Lanier in their balloons. That was the beginning of a yearly event that would obtain millions in free publicity for the area and grow to have thirty to fifty balloons per event. In 2019, it will be the forty-fifth year of the Helen Balloon Race.

The most publicity of any Helen balloon happening came in May 1976. It was the third annual balloon race, and the event had caught on. Balloonists came from everywhere. It was a big deal, with days of partying leading up to lift-off. Everybody was juiced up. It was the time of year it was common to see Pete dressed in his traditional Helen wear for the "in" group. There was the bush jacket with a Helen patch over the pocket, a pair of light-blue jeans, tan, suede shoes, and for Pete, there was a black beret on his head.

He was ready to fly whenever the mood struck him. Stories ran rampant of Pete's flying adventures and near-death landings. His free-spirit life went hand in hand with his Helen project. He relished the challenge and didn't ever worry about losing. On the Saturday before the balloon race, a ballooning adventure such as this took place. It was his way of priming the folks for the big event. This day he would take his writer friend Phil for a simple little afternoon flight. It turned out to be anything but that.

The winds normally blew down the Valley toward Clarkesville, but not on that day. Pete and Phil found themselves flying toward the north side of Lake Burton in a northeastern direction from take-off. Not a good route. It was full of thick mountainsides and had very few good landing sites. On top of that, the weather wasn't too good either.

Somewhere over the far northern part of Lake Burton, Pete fired the balloon: Lanier's Kaleidoscope on that day. He was trying to get a higher altitude in order to change directions for easier access to landing areas. That's when he noticed the top of the balloon was beginning to open, which was about the worst thing that could happen. The hot air would escape, the balloon would begin to fall to the earth, faster and faster, then complete collapse of the envelope, looking like a streamer heading down. No, not a good thing.

Phil said later, Pete told him calmly that it didn't look good and it might be the last flight for both of them. He said, "Just hang on. Enjoy the ride. I'm going to try and climb up in the balloon to get the top closed."

He managed to get it almost back together, and returned to the basket to burn the burners to slow the descent. Just before they hit the tops of the pines, he managed to get everything in better control, resulting in a rough, hard landing. They safely walked away.

Phil later stated the ride wasn't quite what he had in mind when they lifted off. I'm pretty sure it was the last flight he ever took.

The next day, Pete created a party on the fifth fairway of the golf course with food and drink. The giant balloon was repaired and made air worthy for the upcoming race. The top was fixed and I could only think, *This is a good thing.*

I was awakened by Pete pulling on my leg at 6:00 a.m. Wednesday morning. "Get up. I'm going to fly, and I need you to get me the other tank of propane."

Never knowing what to expect out of Pete, I asked no questions and just did what he asked. I headed for his office to gather up the tank, and then toward the fifth fairway, where he was flying. Just as I turned to head across the river, I saw the great, multicolored balloon reach treetop height and disappear over the mountain, heading for Sautee Valley. I headed first to Sautee Valley, then turned left at the Sautee Store on 255 North toward Batesville. I kept a sharp lookout for Pete. Then, I saw him headed toward the trees and preparing to land in a pasture near 255 Alternate.

As he landed, I jumped out of my truck and helped hold the balloon down until it was neutral. Then, I gave Pete the new full tank and took the old one. He replaced it, then turned to face me, saying, "You ready for your first balloon ride?"

I quickly answered, "Sure, why not?" I climbed in.

Up, up, and away, straight through the Valley, gaining altitude as we went. Little did I know this first ride would be the beginning of a whole new experience and the end of another. We gained altitude while heading southeast toward the Hollywood area of Habersham County. I could see my truck getting smaller and smaller. What a feeling! We were moving, but there was no feeling of motion or wind. We were traveling with it. It was as if we had become part of all movement. The only way I could tell there was any wind at all was from looking at the tree leaves turned backward.

We tracked out of the Valley and over the hills of Habersham, heading right down New Liberty Road. We were flying right over property of Pete's, then John Kollock's home place, next Tom and Marion Tidmore's cabin, as well as other things of importance to Pete and his life. Then, we were over Highway 441, flying higher than ever as we headed for Toccoa, Georgia. We flew right over Downtown Toccoa and headed for the shopping centers on Highway 17. Pete dropped altitude so we could wave at the folks below. They just loved that! We also had to start thinking about a landing spot. It was about 9:00 a.m., and the good flying time was nearing an end.

Pete brought us down after crossing Highway 17. We were right at the new motel where the press and TV crews were staying for the upcoming balloon race. We were flying at treetop height, dragging through some large oak trees.

Pete turned and handed me a fresh oak leaf, saying, "I want you to have your first oak leaf. We'll be landing soon."

It was a classic event of ballooning called tree-topping. He told me we would drag out of the trees, then slow down our speed and fly about 150 feet, going over some nearby power lines. Then, we would vent down in the field close beyond for an easy landing. He asked me to gather up the nylon tether rope and be ready to throw it out before landing. It was another standard safety procedure in case there was ground help, which we didn't appear to have.

What did I know? It was my first balloon ride.

I noticed we were picking up speed and Pete was burning the burners more than normal. I just stood there, holding the rope and looking back and forth between him and the fast-approaching eye-level-high power lines. His face showed more and more concern, and the balloon didn't gain altitude. For some reason, there was no lift. The top was in and the burners burned, but still no lift.

Then, out of the blue, Pete said quickly, "Hue, get down the rope!"

Without one word, I turned to face the power lines some twenty feet away, threw out the rope, and jumped over the side, all in one motion. All I knew was I was falling from somewhere up in the sky. I was back first, and the rope was somewhere around me. How long was it going to take me to hit the ground? It was so far and seemed to be taking so long. Then it happened: this unbelievable shock went threw me and everything lit up.

What was that? What had happened?

Then, it stopped. I found myself on the ground on my back. I didn't remember hitting, nor did I know if I had been knocked out. All I knew was I had to be hurt, and bad.

How far had I fallen?

I was afraid to move in case I had a spinal injury, so I laid there for a while. I tried to move my fingers and hands. They worked. Then, I tried my feet and legs. They worked, too. It was time to sit up, which I did. I was still okay. There was no blood. No bones were sticking out. Then, I suddenly lost my breath, but for some reason, I remembered to put my head forward and between my legs, and it worked. I was all right.

I got up, not even muddy. I had landed in a power-line cut that was covered with big briars. How the hell could I be all right?

Then, as I looked around, I could see the broken power lines dancing around. They were shooting fire like giant roman candles. I looked up to see the balloon draped over the power line, like it had wrapped it. It might have. It was then I wondered, *Where's Pete?*

I found him lying on his back nearly directly under the hanging basket. He seemed to be normal, in that there was no blood or outwardly broken bones, but he wouldn't respond. I kept trying to get him to answer me, but it was no use. He was either dead or hurt really badly.

I knew what was left for me to do. I had to get out of this wasteland and get help for Pete and myself. I knew I was hurt and in shock. Everywhere I looked, there was fire from the power lines. The only way out was around and through a creek, and to work my way to a nearby roadway. I had no choice but to do it, so I did.

When I first looked, I didn't see anyone on the road, but when I approached the ten-foot embankment to get up to it, there were multitudes. They were everywhere, including an older police officer. He just watched me try to climb up the bank without offering to help. Finally, he said, "You in that balloon?"

I answered, "Yes. I need some help up this bank, and there's a man out there that's hurt really badly. He needs help quick."

He helped me the rest of the way up the hill. I told him I needed to get to the hospital, because my back was beginning to hurt and I needed care. His answer has always stuck with me. He said, "Just go sit over there." What a dope!

About that time, another, younger policeman approached me, asking if I was in the balloon, and I confirmed, telling him I needed help. He quickly got me by the arm, leading me through the crowd to his patrol car. As he helped me into the front seat, I was attacked by reporters, folks with TV cameras and mics. They were all talking at once and asking questions about the accident. Lucky for me, the policeman shut the door, which provided a shield between me and them.

Then, he took off. Lights, sirens, and everything. He was going so fast through town that I had to ask him to slow down. Come to find out later, he was new on the force. He had just transferred two weeks prior from Decatur, my hometown near Atlanta!

Once at the hospital, they took wonderful care of me. The ER nurse went against rules and provided me with a phone, with which I could call family in Atlanta to let them know I was okay. With all the press coverage, there was no telling what would be on the news. I didn't want them to hear of the accident that way.

The result of my one-night stay in the hospital was I had three broken ribs in my back. Pete was dead on the scene. Efforts were made to keep the FFA investigator away from me in order to give the local investors time to get their story straight for insurance purposes. They thought I might say the wrong thing. My, how folks act when there is a death.

The power company informed me I had fallen about 120 feet from balloon basket to ground. The doctor said the rope burn running under my chin from ear to ear could have been from when the balloon hit the wires. It seems the electrical current traveled down the rope and into me, because I was apparently tangled up at that moment. The blast that hit me during my fall was from the current arching off me, stopping my fall in midair. Once the current broke, I took the blow of the remaining distance. Who knows, it could have been fifty to fifty-five feet. I'll never know.

One thing is pretty clear: if I had taken the full blow of the fall from 120 feet, on my back, it would have been all over for me.

To confirm this, one person saw what happened. He was working in a field, and he said one man looked like he was stopped and hanging in midair. Must have been me. As for Pete, I was told he died from a fat embolism from a leg break. I didn't ask questions.

The funeral came next, and in true Pete fashion, his casket had to be turned up on its end to get him in and out of the church. He would have loved it—anything for more attention. He was buried out off of New Liberty Road in a family plot, the same area we had flown over just two days earlier.

The wake was in Helen, and what a party! Pete would have liked that also. The folks attending didn't have a clue what they had ahead of them without Pete. All I could think about was the first day I met Pete, and he had just returned from a funeral. On this day, it was his funeral.

The balloon race was cancelled and all went home. The accident had resulted in more publicity than the balloon race, putting Helen in front of all America. This time, it wasn't free. We had just paid the dearest price of all: the loss of our leader.

With Pete gone, the ones that were to gain or lose by his death did what I thought they might. They asked me to lie! For insurance purposes, they wanted me to say I was flying the balloon. I said no, and that was the end of that.

After, some people thought they could be our new savior and leader, but that was only in their minds. There wasn't another Pete, nor would there ever be. Each day that passed after his death, the feeling became more numbing as reality set in. We had to take hold, each of us, using what Pete had taught us, along with drawing from the best we had to offer. Most of us did!

What If?

Some things are better left unsaid, but I need to share with each of you something I have lived with ever since Pete's death, and it could be that others share this little bit of a question.

In the previous chapter, I made notice that when the Kaleidoscope balloon was repaired on that day after the Lake Burton mishap, where the top came open, someone said that it's fixed; the top won't come open now. I remember that, and I have wondered about the wisdom of a top that wouldn't come open.

When ballooning and in time of danger, opening the top could save your life. Of course, you don't want it opening during normal flight. Why didn't Pete pop the top when he knew we were going to hit the lines?

Some have said he thought he would gain enough loss of weight when I jumped to make it over the lines, and I might or might not have had a chance to survive. Others say that his gas wasn't hooked up right and we couldn't get lift. Another thought is that the weather changed, temperatures dropped, and winds picked up, making it impossible to get the giant balloon hot enough to climb.

All of these reasons could have been possible, but what if he had chosen to pop the top? We might have both lived.

The answer to that has been said that due to Pete having a plate in his head (from trying to beat a train across a track in Gwinnett County when he was younger), he knew he couldn't take the fall, or any fall. I wonder if he knew there would be a fall, and that it would make no difference what kind of fall.

Maybe popping the top wasn't an option that could have saved his life. I don't know.

The End or Beginning

Sometimes people use the phrase "That was the beginning of the end," but in the case of Pete's death, it was a new, fearful beginning. It was gut-up time for most of us. It was time for the cream to rise to the top. Each of us were forced to take hold, use our talents, and push forward toward our goal of making Alpine Helen a tourist powerhouse in the state of Georgia.

We did just that. Today, Helen is a household name in the tourist industry throughout the South. This was made possible by thousands of folks who, over the years, became part of the Helen story. Most of these folks have gone, either by choice or natural causes. There are a few who still remain, some active, others not so much.

I'm happy to say the success of Helen has continued to be due to the contributions offered by little people with their little dabs of money. Big money never became part of Helen, either in the beginning or in later years. Helen was developed without corporate or government funding, and this fact was always used by Pete in his interviews. Helen was his pride and joy.

As for me, I did my thing in Helen, from business ventures, developing real estate, politics, and serving on about every board possible. I've been praised, awarded, abused, and criticized through the years, and by the mid-1990s I had gotten out of everything and sold all my Helen properties.

I tried. Lord knows, I tried to be uninvolved and make way for the new breed of Helen folks, but things kept happening. I would hear people put off on Helen, and the bristles of pride would stand straight up on the back of my neck. More times than I want to remember, I've had days ruined by thoughtless people making negative comments about something they didn't have a clue about: Helen.

Then, when getting my mail at the Helen post office, I would run into people from the past who had more information than I wanted to process about the current state of affairs in Helen. This was upsetting to me, too. In other words, I couldn't get away from the past. It boiled down to one single fact: hardly anyone understood how Helen came to be, and more importantly, no one understood who created the foundation on which so many folks built and have had a chance to succeed or fail in the Helen game.

The tourists, of course, enjoy the benefits of the efforts from years of giving, working, and preparing put in by the original game players. They flock to our Bavarian village for the enjoyment, and I also know full well not all people like our brand of tourism. That's okay. It would be a horrible world if we all liked the same things. With a little more effort to understand our history, these doubting Thomases might see what we all saw: something special. Most tourists don't have a clue of how Helen became what it is, whether they like Helen or not.

So, I'm proud to say I once again became involved. I was appointed back onto the Helen Chamber of Commerce board, and have served with several others who have aged along with Helen. They are also proud! Today, my goal is to try to help pull Helen together with the people all having a better understanding of one another. I want people to know why we are here—in Helen, that is.

Bingo. This book had to be written. It's been like a skeleton in my closet for over forty years. To me, it's like finally putting Pete to rest by giving him the credit he so truly earned. After he died, the city honored him with a park we called Pete's Park, which was located on the back of Unicoi Hill in Downtown Helen. It was a place for kids to play. From the time it was built, it began to run down until it went *poof*.

Like Pete, forgotten.

Later, in the early eighties, Doctor Tom Tidmore and I had a plaque made in memory of Pete to be placed on the inside wall of the Festhalle in Helen. Tom made the presentation in a packed house on Saturday afternoon to the Oktoberfest crowd. Lanier and Chris flew away in the original Swiss cross Helen balloon, and at the same time, Winston, Roy, and I lifted off for the first free flight of a brand-new Spirit of Helen balloon. The results were, the old balloon had its last flight due to a horrible accident that day where Lanier and Chris were both critically injured. We landed in a horse pasture in Sky Lake. That was the last ballooning for me. I retired from flying with my best landing ever. Always quit while you're at your peak. The plaque was not seen again until the fall of 2003, when it was found in the attic of the same Festhalle.

A memorial to Pete has been hard to come by . . . unless you stand back on one of the hills overlooking Helen and think about what you're seeing. Then, consider the soon-to-be forty-nine years of Oktoberfest and forty-five years of balloon races. Think of where it all started, what those two events have done, and what part they have played in the region. Look back to when Helen was a sleepy little ghost town versus what it has become today. There is no comparison.

Yes, Pete was a dreamer, but he had a knack that most dreamers don't have: he could make his dreams come true.

When you look again at Helen, remember it's real. It was Pete's dream which came into being. The memorials to him may not have lasted, but I think they were too small anyway. Alpine Helen itself is a much more appropriate and everlasting memorial.

Festhalle rededicated to the late Pete Hodgkinson

By MELISSA WINDER
White County News-Telegraph

A polka band, guests in German attire and Hurricane Ivan gathered at the Festhalle Thursday night for the Oktoberfest kickoff.

In addition to drinking and dancing, a rededication of the Festhalle was the main event.

The structure was dedicated to the late Pete Hodgkinson, an original promoter and developer of Alpine Helen. In his dedication, Hue Rainey referred to Hodgkinson as a dreamer and visionary who led Helen to happen.

Hodgkinson began dreaming up his ideas for Helen in 1973. He died three years later in the Helen to Atlantic balloon race. Rainey said when Hodgkinson began Oktoberfest, it consisted of a keg of beer on the back of a pickup truck.

However, Hodgkinson did get to see the now almost eight-week-long festival grow.

Hodgkinson took the Helen community to one of the top five tourist areas in the state, Rainey said. The original dedication to Hodgkinson was to take place in the mid-1980s but somewhere in between the plaque was misplaced.

Volunteers found the plaque this year, and Rainey said it was now time to finish the rededication.

Another recognition was given to Ingrid Tyre for refurbishing murals inside and outside the Festhalle.

Hodgkinson's plaque can be seen in the Festhalle. Oktoberfest will continue through Saturday, Nov. 6.

Hue Rainey hangs up the rediscovered plaque which dedicates the Festhalle to the late Pete Hodkinson. Hodkinson was a leading visionary of Alpine Helen. The hall was originally planned to be dedicated to Hodkinson in the 1980s, but the plaque was misplaced. (Staff photo/Melissa Winder)

About the Author

Hue Rainey had the good fortune at age fifteen to live in Germany, a life-changing experience. Later, in his early thirties, he had the additional good fortune of being given the opportunity to be a leader in the early development of Alpine Helen. This, too, was a life-changing adventure.

Hue retired in the mid-1990s to Sautee Nacoochee, where he, his wife, Jane, and two dogs, Zoey and Corky, live overlooking their vineyard and the historical Nacoochee Valley.

Although retired, Hue has a passion to share the inside truth of how Alpine Helen came to succeed and how it continues to play a major role in Georgia tourism. Through this shared knowledge, he hopes it will also be life-changing for the readers.